Grandmother's
FAVORITE
QUILTS™

Edited by Sandra L. Hatch

HOUSE of
WHITE
BIRCHES
PUBLISHERS
SINCE 1947

Grandmother's Favorite Quilts

Editor: Sandra L. Hatch
Copy Editor: Cathy Reef
Assistant to Editorial Director: Jeanne Stauffer
Editorial Director: Vivian Rothe

Photography: Nora Elsesser, Tammy Christian, Rhonda Davis
Photography Assistant: Linda Quinlan

Creative Coordinator: Shaun Venish
Production Manager: Vicki Macy
Technical Artist: Connie Rand
Production Artist: Brenda Gallmeyer
Production Coordinator: Sandra Ridgway Beres
Production Assistant: Cheryl Lynch

Publishers: Carl H. Muselman, Arthur K. Muselman
Chief Executive Officer: John Robinson
Marketing Director: Scott Moss

Printed in the United States of America
First Printing: 1995
Library of Congress Number: 95-77647
ISBN: 1-882138-12-0

Every effort has been made to ensure the accuracy and completeness of the instructions in this book. However, we cannot be responsible for human error or for the results when using materials other than those specified in the instructions, or for variations in individual work.

Cover quilt: *Sunshine & Shadow*, pattern begins on Page 49.

Quilted Memories
❧ of Yesterday ❧

Our grandmothers grew up and lived in a very different era than we do. History books tell us how women in the 1920s began to find leisure time because of advances in industrialization. Manufactured goods could be purchased locally or through mail-order catalogs. Women could buy fabric produced in textile mills right here in the United States.

During this time of change, many men were able to find jobs with a steady paycheck every week, and families became accustomed to purchasing goods. Women no longer needed to make warm quilts as their grandmothers did in the pioneer days.

Just when people had settled into this new way of life, the bottom fell out when the stock market crashed. The lifestyle to which many had become accustomed was to be no more.

Quiltmaking became a necessity again, and quilters used whatever was at hand to make quilts. Were these quilts depressing and dark? No, we view them as bright and colorful. It is hard to believe many of these quilts were made during difficult times.

One major influence on quilts made in the early '30s was the contest sponsored by Sears & Roebuck for the 1933 World's Fair. Twenty-five thousand quilts were finished and entered in regional contests, with the winners being hung at the fair in Chicago for almost six months.

The winning prize was a huge sum for that time, $1,200 for the first prize, with more than $7,500 in all given away for the other top quilts. Converted to today's economy that sum equals about $20,000. During the Depression, this sum could provide food for many months. Every quilter wanted to participate and win that fabulous prize.

For many years quilt collectors overlooked quilts made in the 20th century, because they were more interested in the older quilts. In recent years, however, quilts from this era have become very collectible, and the prices have reflected this change of attitude.

Many of the popular quilt patterns used today were created during our grandmothers' early days. Newspapers and magazines printed patterns in every issue. Many women collected these patterns with the thought of one day using them to make quilts.

We have collected patterns for some of those wonderful designs to include in this book: *Grandmother's Flower Garden, Double Wedding Ring, Sunbonnet Sue* and many more. Most of the quilts shown were completed in the 1930s and use fabrics typical of that time. Cotton prints with white backgrounds, flour and sugar sacks, feed sacks and that unusual solid green color are evident in many of the quilts.

These beautiful antique quilts exude only happy thoughts even though they were often stitched in troubling times. This book is a tribute to the women who made those lovely quilts and those who have cherished and taken care of them so we can still appreciate them today.

❧ Contents ❧

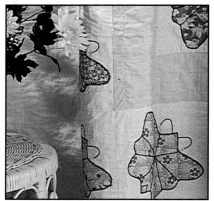

❧Contents❧

Block Piecing

Pieced quilts are more abundant than any other type. Most of these quilts are made up of individually pieced blocks which are set together in a variety of ways.

Quilt patterns were plentiful in the 1930s, with many newspapers printing patterns on a regular basis. The Kansas City Star printed almost 1,000 designs between 1928 and 1961, some of them repeated with different names.

These beautiful patterns are still treasured and used by quiltmakers today. You'll find 12 all-time favorites on the following pages.

Tips & Techniques for

❧ Block Piecing ❧

Most pieced quilts are made up of individually pieced blocks which are then arranged in a number of ways, called settings. The result is a wide variety of quilt designs, which can look dramatically different depending on which setting you choose. You'll find more information to help you with this step of quiltmaking on Pages 163 and 164.

We have selected block-pieced quilts from the 1930s that are examples of a number of settings. You can put them together as shown in the photos of the actual quilts, or use a setting idea from another quilt. Just because the instructions tell you to set them one way doesn't mean you have to do it that way. Go out on a limb and try something different with your blocks. Grandmother would encourage you to do just that!

Block Piecing Tips. Always make one sample block to try out the pattern. This will help you decide exactly what fabric and colors you like best, and give you a chance to work with any piecing techniques that are new to you.

• The first number given on a template reflects the number to cut for one block. The number in parentheses is the number to cut to make the quilt as shown.

• The measurements given in Placement Diagrams indicate the finished size. Figure drawings show pieces with seam allowance included.

Making Your Border. Border-strip sizes are given for the exact size needed if all stitching is perfect.

• After you have pieced your quilt top, be sure to measure the size of the quilt, referring to the instructions given on Page 164.

• The measurements given include a 1/4" seam allowance all around. For example, a border strip that finishes to 2" would be cut 2 1/2".

• If yardage is not long enough to cut border strips the length needed, piece strips to make the desired size. It is preferable to use a one-piece strip, but sometimes that means buying 3 yards of fabric just to cut four border strips.

Color Selection. If you are a beginner, study the photos of the completed quilts. Your reaction to them will guide you in your color choices.

• Nature's color wheel can teach us what colors work. Look outside at the green trees, blue sky and the colors on the horizon. Study wildflowers in fields and see how the colors work together.

Fabric for Scrap Quilts. Although each pattern has a list of materials needed to construct the quilt as shown, you probably already have lots of fabric on hand. Most fabric shops sell quarter-yard pieces, fat quarters (18" x 22") or even fat eighths (9" x 18"). Some shops bundle chosen fabrics in coordinating sets that look attractive. These bundles can be used to make some very interesting quilts.

Be sure to read General Instructions for Quiltmaking, beginning on Page 152, for more tips and techniques to help you in constructing your quilt.

Zigzagging Japanese Fans

Fan quilts offer a note of nostalgia to most of us since many of our grandmothers saved scraps from clothing to make a fan quilt for a lucky daughter. Fan patterns were very popular in the 1930s and date back to the Crazy Quilt era of the 1870s and before. Quilters today are still enchanted by the fan and its lovely related shapes.

This simple fan pattern has only three blades, but each blade has two parts. The placement of the fans creates a diagonal design that at first glance doesn't resemble a fan shape. Try several other arrangements with these blocks before joining them in rows. You may find another design that suits you better.

Instructions

Step 1. Prepare templates and cut as directed for one block (whole quilt), referring to Pages 154 and 155 for instructions.

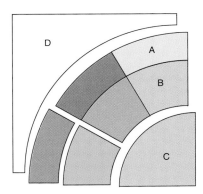

Figure 1
Piece block as shown.

Quilt Measurements	
Quilt Size: 70" x 91"	**Block Size:** 7" x 7"

Materials
• 3 yards muslin
• Variety of print scraps
• Backing 74" x 95"
• Batting 74" x 95"
• 9 1/4 yards self-made or purchased binding

Step 2. To piece one block, referring to Figure 1, sew A to B three times; join to make arch shape. Set in C; set on D; press.

Step 3. Repeat for 130 blocks.

Step 4. Arrange the pieced blocks in 13 rows of 10 blocks each referring to the Placement Diagram.

Note: *Experiment with alternate placements to make an entirely different design.*

Step 5. Join the blocks in rows; join the rows to complete the pieced top and press.

Tips & Techniques

Remember that when sewing convex and concave shapes like pieces C and D, careful pinning of seams to ease in bulk will help (Figure 2). Sometimes the inside seams require clipping to allow them to stretch enough for the pieces to fit together. This depends on the amount of curve—the deeper the curve, the more likely it is that you will need to clip seams, as shown in Figure 3.

Step 6. Choose a quilt design and mark on the completed top referring to Page 167.

Step 7. Finish the quilt as desired referring to Pages 167–175.

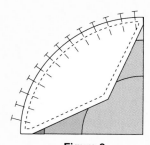

Figure 2
Ease the excess on concave pieces
by placing pins very close together
as shown.

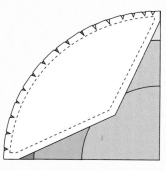

Figure 3
Clip very deep concave seam allowances
when sewing seam.

Place line on fold

D
Cut 1 muslin (130)

A
Cut 3 scraps (390)

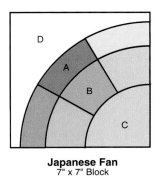

Japanese Fan
7" x 7" Block

Zigzagging Japanese Fans
Placement Diagram
70" x 91"

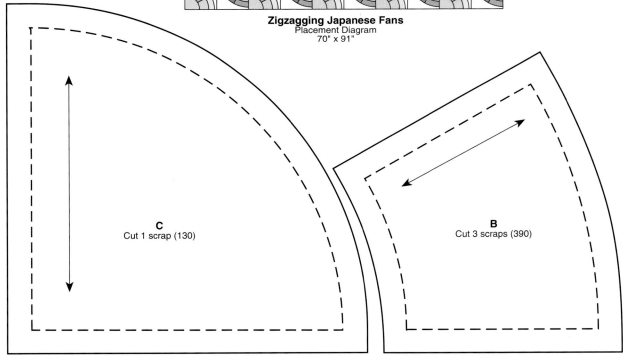

C
Cut 1 scrap (130)

B
Cut 3 scraps (390)

Razz-Ma-Tazz

Yard sales sometimes yield precious finds. This eight-pointed star quilt top was one of four found at one sale. Because some of the fabrics were repeated in each top, it would appear that they were all pieced by the same person. She must have liked to piece, but did not like to quilt! The top was set together in rows alternating unpieced print blocks with pieced ones.

Finding a quilt top with no history is sad. We could conjure up a story about the tops found at the yard sale using the available clues. The fabrics belonged to the period between the 1930s and 1950s. The later quilt tops weren't pieced as well as the earlier ones. This could indicate that the maker's eyesight was failing. She also used brighter colors each time, probably for the same reason.

It may be that this quilt top was the last one she made and is the wildest one of the bunch. It's so happy and cheerful, it was named *Razz-Ma-Tazz*.

Some of the blocks are a little uneven in the piecing, but it doesn't make the quilt any less appealing. It speaks of someone who loved quilting right up to the very end. We all hope to have the courage and good sense to keep quilting long after we can't see anymore!

Instructions

Step 1. To complete one block as shown in Figure 1, sew a light A to a dark A. Repeat for all A pieces. Sew the dark B's to the medium BRs. Set the A-A squares into the B-BR units referring to Pages 155–157 for instructions. Arrange these units to make block corners and sew together on B sides. Set in C all around to complete the block; press.

Quilt Measurements
Quilt Size: 64" x 80"   **Block Size:** 8" x 8"

Materials
• 2 yards yellow print fabric • Scraps for blocks • Batting 68" x 84" • Backing 68" x 84" • 8 yards self-made or purchased binding

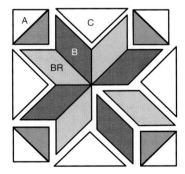

Figure 1
Piece block units as shown.

Step 2. Piece 40 blocks to complete the quilt top as shown.

Step 3. Cut the yellow print fabric into 40 squares 8 1/2" x 8 1/2".

Step 4. Arrange the pieced blocks with the yellow print squares referring to the Placement Diagram.

Step 5. Sew together in 10 rows consisting of four pieced and four yellow print squares. Join the rows to complete the quilt top; press.

Step 6. Borders may be added at this time to make a larger quilt, if desired.

Step 7. Choose a quilting design or design one of your own. Mark the design on the top referring to the instructions given on Page 167.

Step 8. Finish quilt referring to Pages 167–175 for instructions.

Razz-Ma-Tazz
8" x 8" Block

Tips & Techniques

In days gone by one could purchase grain in feed sacks made from fabric. Other commodities were sold in fabric sacks as well. After the contents were used up, the sacks or bags were washed and saved to be used for other things including clothing and quilts.

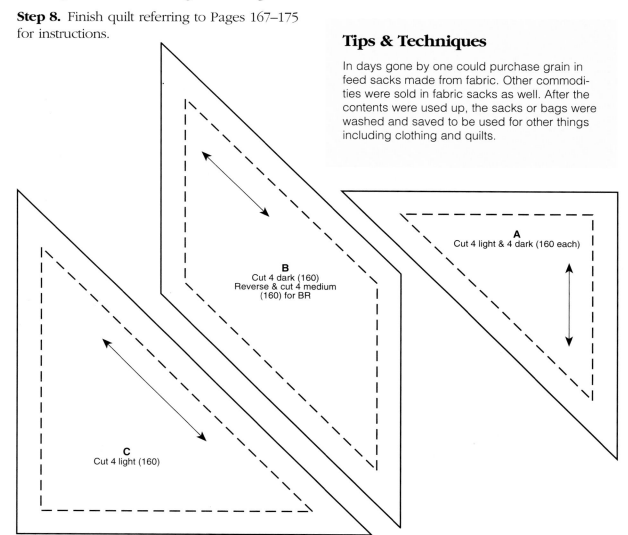

B
Cut 4 dark (160)
Reverse & cut 4 medium
(160) for BR

A
Cut 4 light & 4 dark (160 each)

C
Cut 4 light (160)

Razz-Ma-Tazz
Placement Diagram
64" x 80"

Scrappy Triangles

One of the things that is so wonderful about old quilts is the way every little scrap was used. If you have some scraps from your grandmother's day, make them up into an heirloom-quality quilt using this easy pattern.

The quilt top shown uses scraps of five lovely pastel colors in blocks separated by sashing strips, giving each block a chance to be noticed. Pink, yellow, peach, blue and pale green fabrics were the predominant colors used in the prints found in quilts of the 1930s.

Instructions

Step 1. To piece one block, sew a print B to a solid B eight times; sew together to form squares referring to Figure 1. Join B units with A as shown in Figure 2.

Quilt Measurements
Quilt Size: 72" x 102"   **Block Size:** 12" x 12"

Materials
• Scraps of contrasting prints and solids • 2 1/2 yards sashing fabric • Backing 76" x 106" • Batting 76" x 106" • 10 yards self-made or purchased binding

Figure 1
Sew 2 B pieces together as shown.

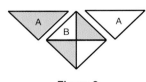

Figure 2
Join B units with A.

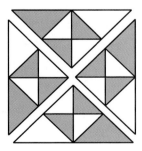

Figure 3
Piece block units as shown.

Step 2. Repeat three times; sew resulting triangles together referring to Figure 3 to complete one block. Repeat for 35 blocks.

Step 3. Cut six sashing strips 3 1/2" x 72 1/2". From the remaining sashing fabric, cut 28 sashing strips 3 1/2" x 12 1/2".

Step 4. Arrange the blocks with the sashing strips referring to the Placement Diagram. Join in rows; join the rows with the long strips to complete the top.

Step 5. Borders may be added if desired and quilt may be finished in your favorite method referring to Pages 164–175.

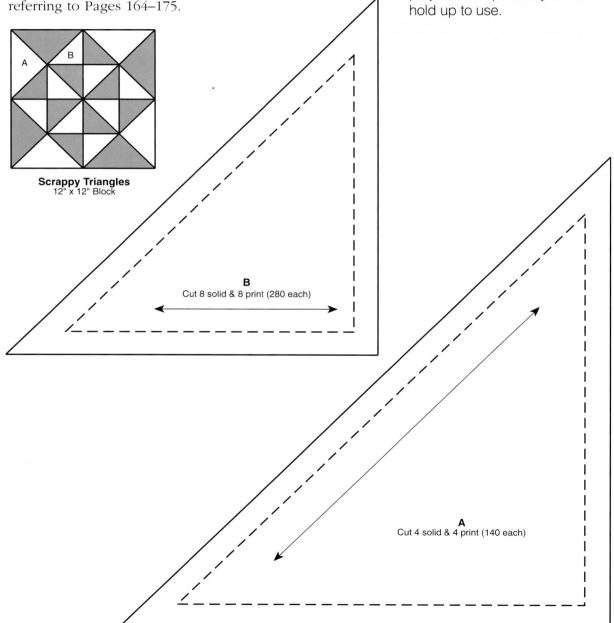

Scrappy Triangles
12" x 12" Block

B
Cut 8 solid & 8 print (280 each)

A
Cut 4 solid & 4 print (140 each)

Tips & Techniques

Grandmother's thread is fun to collect, but don't use it on any of your sewing or quilting projects as it probably won't hold up to use.

Scrappy Triangles
Placement Diagram
72" x 102"

Pinwheel Baby Quilt

Making a scrap quilt for Baby is easy with this simple Pinwheel design. Search through your scrap bag and use up some of your favorites on this crib-size quilt. What better gift for that new little grandchild than a quilt to keep Baby snug and warm!

Triangles make up the squares and can be cut from scraps using templates or quicker methods. Whatever method you choose, this old-time pattern is a joy to stitch for that special little loved one.

Instructions

Step 1. Use pattern given to cut triangles as directed from scrap fabrics.

Step 2. Join light and dark triangles four times to make triangle/square units referring to Figure 1.

Figure 1
Sew 2 triangle units together to piece 1 unit.

Figure 2
Join 4 units to complete 1 block.

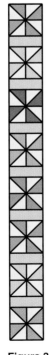

Figure 3
Join 8 blocks with sashing strips as shown.

Quilt Measurements
Quilt Size: 40 1/2" x 46 1/2"
Block Size: 4 1/2" x 4 1/2"

Materials
• Assorted dark and light print scraps for triangles in blocks
• 2 yards pink stripe for sashing and borders
• Embroidery floss or yarn for tying
• Backing 44" x 50"
• Batting 44" x 50"
• 5 yards self-made or purchased binding

Step 3. Join four triangle/square units to complete one block referring to Figure 2. Complete 48 blocks; press.

Step 4. On the lengthwise grain of the sashing fabric, cut five sashing strips 2" x 47"; set aside. Cut two border strips 3 1/2" x 47"; set aside. From the remaining fabric, cut 42 short sashing strips 2" x 5".

Step 5. Arrange the blocks in six rows of eight blocks each. Rearrange the blocks in a pleasing manner. Sew lengthwise rows of eight blocks together with sashing strips between; begin and end with a block referring to Figure 3. Repeat for six rows; press seams toward sashing strips.

Step 6. Join the pieced rows with the 2" x 47" sashing strips; press seams toward strips.

Step 7. Sew the 3 1/2" border strips to the long sides.

Step 8. Prepare quilt top for tying referring to Page 167 for instructions.

Step 9. Bind edges to finish referring to Pages 167–175 for instructions and choices.

Tips & Techniques

The *Pinwheel Baby Quilt* is the perfect project for trying your hand at rotary-cutting and quick-piecing if you will be using a planned color scheme instead of scraps.

The strips are cut 3 1/8" and then cut into 3 1/8" segments. Cut the squares on the diagonal to make triangles. Piece triangles as for traditional methods to complete the triangle/square units.

The maker of the *Pinwheel Baby Quilt* really made use of her scraps. The backing was made with crazy-pieced blocks.

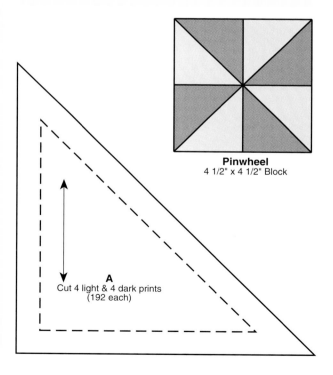

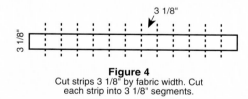

Figure 4
Cut strips 3 1/8" by fabric width. Cut
each strip into 3 1/8" segments.

Figure 5
Cut each square on the
diagonal to make triangles.

Pinwheel
4 1/2" x 4 1/2" Block

A
Cut 4 light & 4 dark prints
(192 each)

Pinwheel Baby Quilt
Placement Diagram
40 1/2" x 46 1/2"

Flower Basket

The pieced quilt top shown here uses all pieced blocks instead of solid blocks between as in the Fruit Basket Quilt shown on Page 30. Half- and quarter-blocks are used to complete the design. The lavender solid fabric used as the basket bases was commonly used in our grandmothers' quilts. If bordered with a similar lavender fabric and quilted, this top could be beautiful.

Using portions of pieced blocks makes this quilt a bit confusing to piece. Begin by piecing the 78 whole blocks. It would be a simple matter to add whole blocks to the edges and then square it off, but it would be such a waste of time and materials to do so.

Although it seems confusing, refer to the Figure drawings and the Placement Diagram to piece the top, side and bottom half-blocks and the two corner units.

Instructions

Step 1. Prepare templates and cut fabric patches as directed on Pages 154 and 155. Quick-cutting and piecing methods may be used; refer to Page 157.

Step 2. Piece one block referring to Figure 1; press. Repeat for 78 whole blocks.

Quilt Measurements	
Quilt Size: 78" x 84"	**Block Size:** 8 1/2" x 8 1/2"

Materials
• 4 yards muslin
• 2 yards lavender solid
• Print scraps 5" x 9 1/2" for each basket
• Backing 84" x 88"
• Batting 84" x 88"
• 9 1/2 yards self-made or purchased binding

Step 3. Piece six bottom half-blocks and six top half-blocks referring to Figure 2; press.

Note: *The bottom half of the block is used on the top row of the quilt; the top half of the block is used on the bottom row of the quilt. The units*

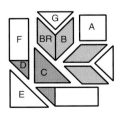

Figure 1
Piece 1 block as shown.

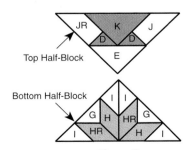

Figure 2
Piece 6 bottom half-blocks and 6 top half-blocks as shown.

are labeled as they are placed on the quilt, not with the part of the block used. Refer to the Figure drawings and the Placement Diagram when placing the block portions.

Step 4. Piece 13 side blocks, reversing six, referring to Figure 3.

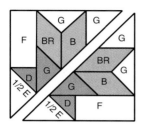

Figure 3
Piece 13 side blocks.
Reverse 6 as shown.

Step 5. Piece one top corner and one bottom corner unit referring to Figure 4.

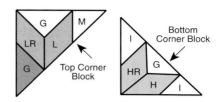

Figure 4
Piece 1 top corner and 1 bottom corner
block as shown.

Step 6. Arrange half- and whole blocks referring to Figure 5. Join blocks in diagonal rows; join the rows and add corner units to complete the top; press.

Step 7. Borders may be added at this time as desired to make the quilt fit a chosen size.

Step 8. Finish quilt referring to Pages 167–175 for instructions.

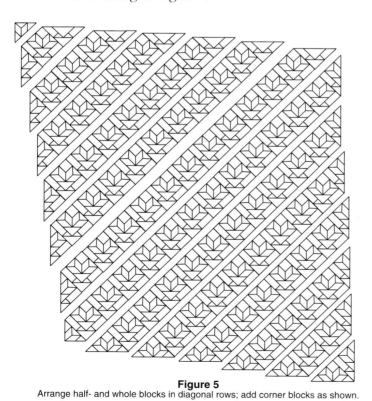

Figure 5
Arrange half- and whole blocks in diagonal rows; add corner blocks as shown.

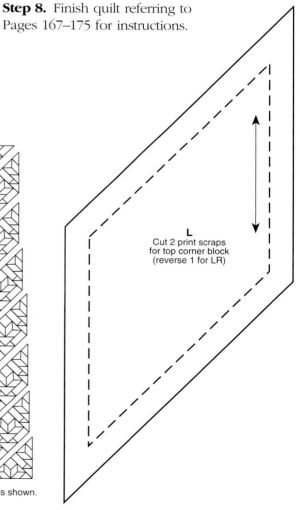

L
Cut 2 print scraps
for top corner block
(reverse 1 for LR)

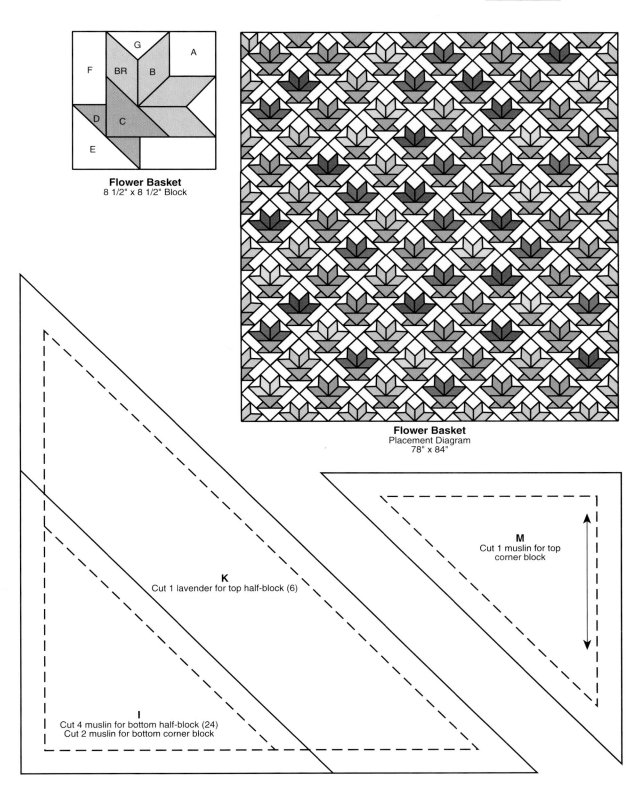

Flower Basket
8 1/2" x 8 1/2" Block

Flower Basket
Placement Diagram
78" x 84"

K
Cut 1 lavender for top half-block (6)

I
Cut 4 muslin for bottom half-block (24)
Cut 2 muslin for bottom corner block

M
Cut 1 muslin for top
corner block

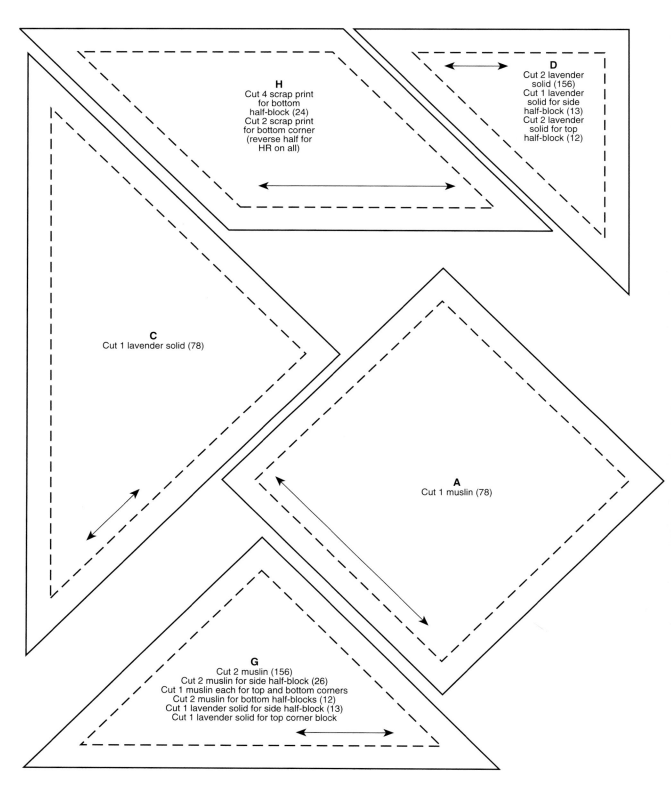

H
Cut 4 scrap print
for bottom
half-block (24)
Cut 2 scrap print
for bottom corner
(reverse half for
HR on all)

D
Cut 2 lavender
solid (156)
Cut 1 lavender
solid for side
half-block (13)
Cut 2 lavender
solid for top
half-block (12)

C
Cut 1 lavender solid (78)

A
Cut 1 muslin (78)

G
Cut 2 muslin (156)
Cut 2 muslin for side half-block (26)
Cut 1 muslin each for top and bottom corners
Cut 2 muslin for bottom half-blocks (12)
Cut 1 lavender solid for side half-block (13)
Cut 1 lavender solid for top corner block

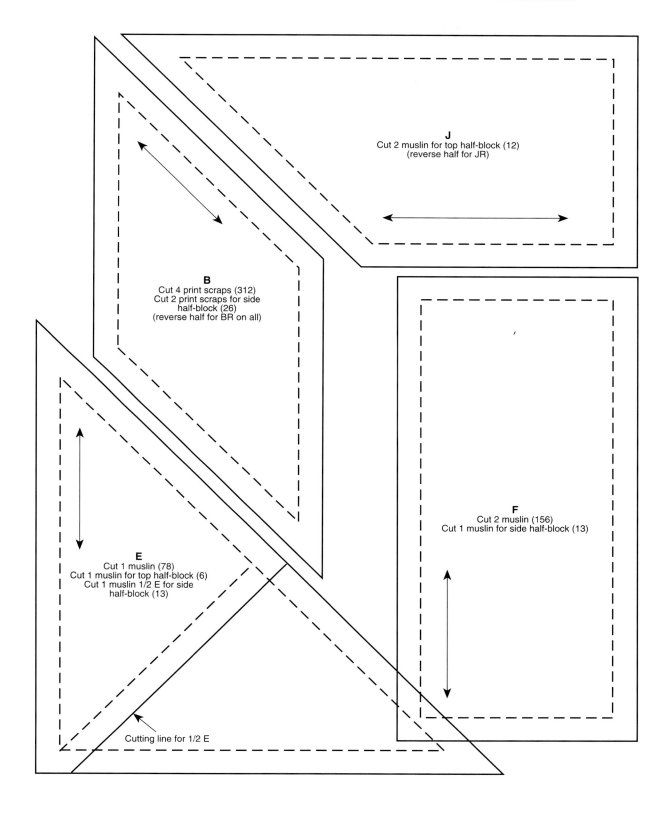

J
Cut 2 muslin for top half-block (12)
(reverse half for JR)

B
Cut 4 print scraps (312)
Cut 2 print scraps for side
half-block (26)
(reverse half for BR on all)

F
Cut 2 muslin (156)
Cut 1 muslin for side half-block (13)

E
Cut 1 muslin (78)
Cut 1 muslin for top half-block (6)
Cut 1 muslin 1/2 E for side
half-block (13)

Cutting line for 1/2 E

Fruit Basket

Fabric baskets are favorites among quilters, as evidenced by the variety of basket patterns created in the 1930s. The Fruit Basket design is known by several other names, the most common being the Cake Stand. The amount of quilting on this basket quilt shows that the grandmother who made this treasured heirloom loved to quilt.

The pieced blocks in this old-time quilt from our grandmothers' era are combined with solid blocks set on point. Each basket uses a different print combined with bleached muslin background pieces to complete the design.

Instructions

Step 1. Cut two muslin strips 6 1/2" x 86" and two strips 6 1/2" x 64" for borders. Set aside.

Step 2. Prepare and cut templates as directed referring to Pages 154 and 155 for instructions.

Step 3. Piece one block by sewing a muslin C to a print C six times. Join three C units twice. Arrange with remaining pieces and join referring to Figure 1. Repeat for 42 blocks; press.

Quilt Measurements
Quilt Size: Approximately 73 3/4" x 83 5/8"
Block Size: 7" x 7"

Materials
• 5 1/2 yards bleached muslin
• 42 print scraps 10" square for blocks
• Print scraps for border triangles
• Backing 76" x 90"
• Batting 76" x 90"
• 12 yards self-made or purchased binding

Step 4. Cut 30 muslin squares 7 1/2" x 7 1/2".

Step 5. Cut six muslin squares 11 1/8" x 11 1/8". Cut apart on both diagonals to make side fill-in triangles referring to Figure 2. Cut two muslin squares 5 7/8" x 5 7/8". Cut once on the diagonal to make corner triangles referring to Figure 2.

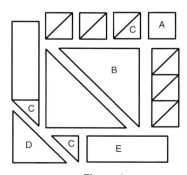

Figure 1
Join the pieces as shown to
complete 1 block.

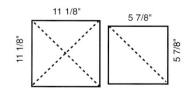

Figure 2
Cut side fill-in and corner triangles as shown.

Step 6. Arrange the pieced blocks with the muslin squares and triangles in diagonal rows referring to Figure 3. Join in rows; join the rows to complete the center pieced section; press.

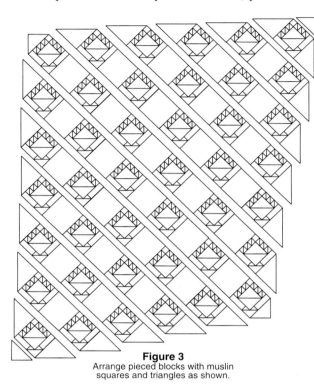

Figure 3
Arrange pieced blocks with muslin
squares and triangles as shown.

Step 7. Sew 25 print F's to 24 muslin F's as shown in Figure 4; repeat. Sew a strip to the top and bottom of quilt center; press seams toward border strips.

Note: *Adjust these strips to fit, if necessary.*

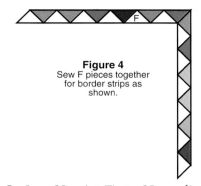

Figure 4
Sew F pieces together
for border strips as
shown.

Step 8. Sew 29 print F's to 28 muslin F's to make a long strip; repeat. Sew a strip to each long side of quilt center; press.

Step 9. Sew the 6 1/2" x 64" muslin border strips to the top and bottom. Press seams toward border strips. Trim excess square at edges. Sew the 6 1/2" x 86" muslin border strips to sides. Press seams toward border strips. Trim excess square at corners.

Step 10. Using the scallop border pattern given and starting in the center of each side border strip, mark the shape on the quilt's edges using a water-erasable marker or pencil. Trim to curved shape. Using a plate of desired size, trace circle shape at corners and trim.

Step 11. Mark the quilting designs given on quilt top referring to Page 167.

Step 12. Finish quilt referring to Pages 167–175.

Note: *Use bias binding to finish the curved edges of the quilt as it will stretch around the border scallops.*

Tips & Techniques

Hand-quilting can produce very sore fingers and strain to muscles in the hand, arm and shoulder. To prevent sore fingers, use a thimble. The finger that is under the quilt to feel the needle as it passes through the backing is the one that is most apt to get sore from the pinpricks. Some quilters purchase leather thimbles for this finger while others try home remedies. One simple aid is masking tape wrapped around the finger. With the tape you will still be able to feel the needle, but it will not prick your skin. Over time calluses build up and these fingers get toughened up, but with every vacation from quilting, they will become soft and the process begins again.

6" x 83 5/8"

6" x 61 3/4"

Fruit Basket
Placement Diagram
Approximately 73 3/4" x 83 5/8"

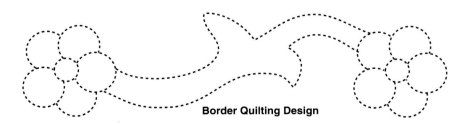

Border Quilting Design

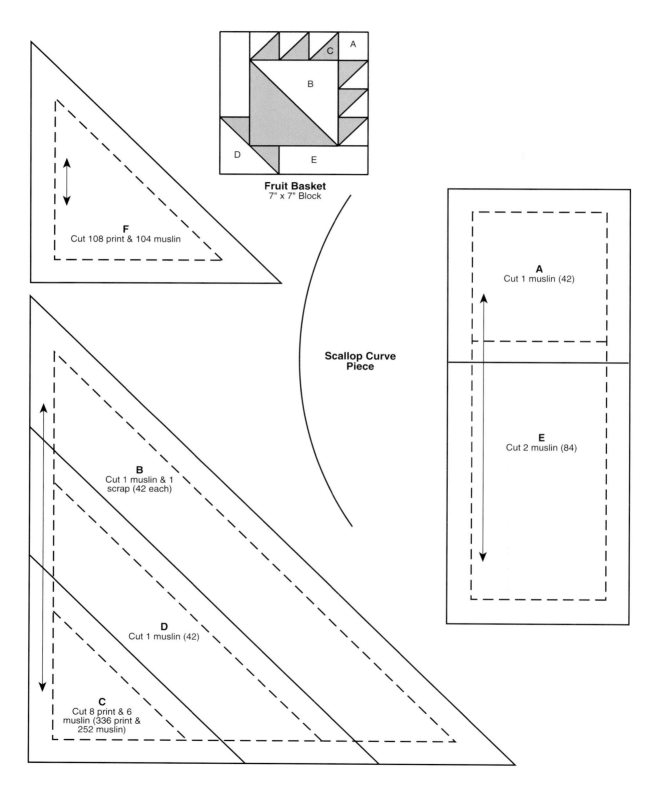

Fruit Basket
7" x 7" Block

F
Cut 108 print & 104 muslin

Scallop Curve Piece

B
Cut 1 muslin & 1 scrap (42 each)

D
Cut 1 muslin (42)

C
Cut 8 print & 6 muslin (336 print & 252 muslin)

A
Cut 1 muslin (42)

E
Cut 2 muslin (84)

Quilting Design for Muslin Blocks

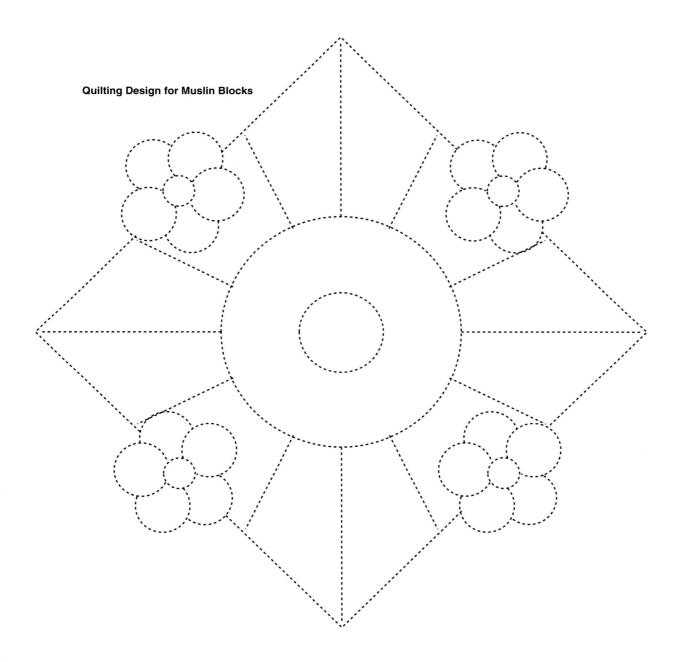

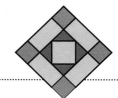

Grandmother's Square in a Square

Stripes and plaids were often used in our grandmothers' quilts.
Colorful and creative, the quilt shown is a wonderful example of the
"use it up and wear it out" philosophy of our grandparents.

This design is an old favorite to piece whether using traditional or faster methods. It has a diagonal set using sashing strips and sections of the pieced blocks on the edges. You'll enjoy working with your collection of scraps to match this old-time pattern.

Instructions

Step 1. Begin piecing by sewing four C's to D. Add B to two opposite sides of this unit. Piece A to B to A twice. Lay out the three rows and sew together to complete one block as shown in Figure 1. Repeat for 28 blocks.

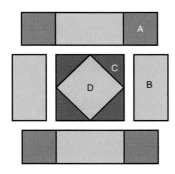

Figure 1
Piece block units as shown.

Step 2. Piece a half-block by sewing 1/2 A to B to A and 1/2 A to B. Sew C to 1/2 D and add 1/2 C on each end. Arrange the pieced units referring to Figure 2 and sew. Repeat for 15 half-blocks for sides and corners.

Quilt Measurements
Quilt Size: Approximately 68" x 78" **Block Size:** 10" x 10"

Materials
• Scraps of stripe material • 2 3/4 yards sashing fabric • Backing 72" x 87" • Batting 72" x 87" • 8 1/4 yards self-made or purchased binding

Step 3. Complete a quarter-block by sewing 1/2 A to B to 1/2 A. Sew 1/2 C to 1/4 D to 1/2 C. Repeat for two quarter-blocks for corners, referring to Figure 3.

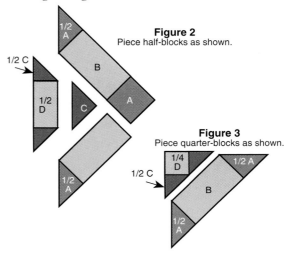

Figure 2
Piece half-blocks as shown.

Figure 3
Piece quarter-blocks as shown.

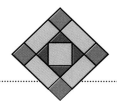

Step 4. Cut 36 sashing strips 2 1/2" x 10 1/2". Cut one of each strip size as follows: 2 1/2" x 15", 2 1/2" x 39", 2 1/2" x 63", 2 1/2" x 87", 2 1/2" x 99", 2 1/2" x 79", 2 1/2" x 52" and 2 1/2" x 28".

Note: *The longer sashing strips will be longer than necessary. When the top is stitched, trim the excess square with edges, using a ruler to draw lines for cutting.*

Step 5. Arrange blocks with sashing strips referring to Figure 4. Join in diagonal rows; press.

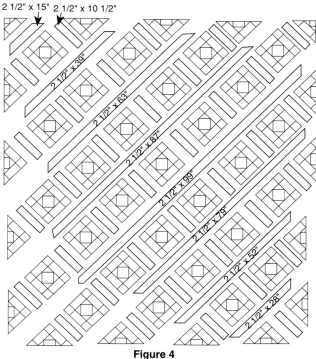

Figure 4
Arrange the blocks with the sashing strips as shown.
Measurements include seam allowances.

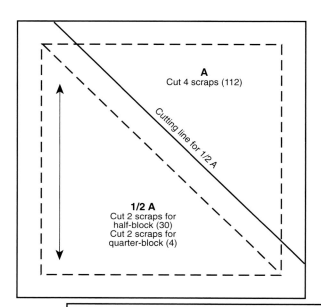

A
Cut 4 scraps (112)

Cutting line for 1/2 A

1/2 A
Cut 2 scraps for half-block (30)
Cut 2 scraps for quarter-block (4)

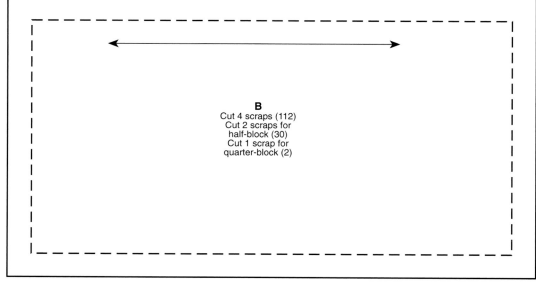

B
Cut 4 scraps (112)
Cut 2 scraps for half-block (30)
Cut 1 scrap for quarter-block (2)

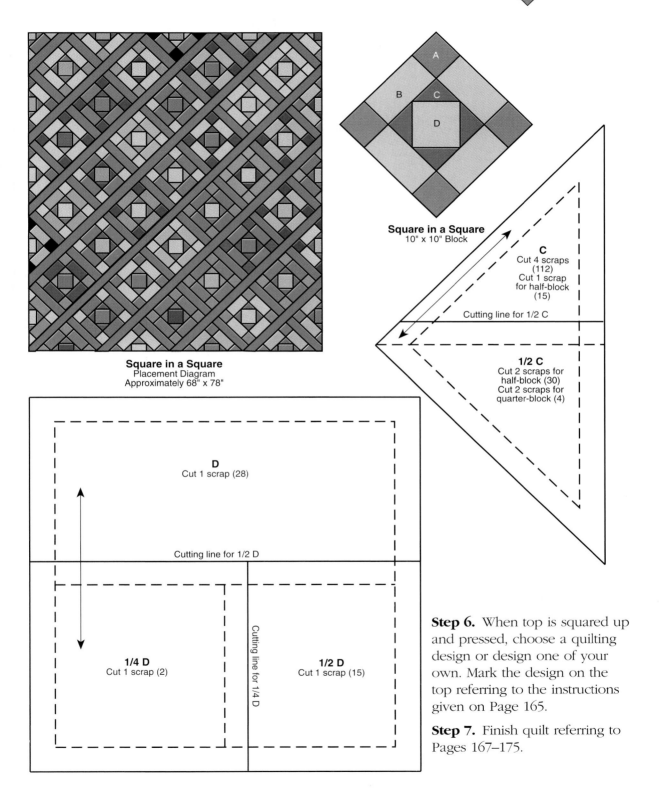

Square in a Square
Placement Diagram
Approximately 68" x 78"

Square in a Square
10" x 10" Block

C
Cut 4 scraps
(112)
Cut 1 scrap
for half-block
(15)

Cutting line for 1/2 C

1/2 C
Cut 2 scraps for
half-block (30)
Cut 2 scraps for
quarter-block (4)

D
Cut 1 scrap (28)

Cutting line for 1/2 D

Cutting line for 1/4 D

1/4 D
Cut 1 scrap (2)

1/2 D
Cut 1 scrap (15)

Step 6. When top is squared up and pressed, choose a quilting design or design one of your own. Mark the design on the top referring to the instructions given on Page 165.

Step 7. Finish quilt referring to Pages 167–175.

Snowball

No doubt the grandmother who stitched this fascinating pattern had a sunny seat by the window where she could watch all the neighborhood children playing in the snow. Notice how the snowball theme is carried into the scalloped border, a clever finishing touch!

Hand-pieced and hand-quilted in the 1930s, this quilt contains a pleasing assortment of floral prints and pastel solids. When the blocks are joined together, perfect round snowball shapes are formed, thus giving the quilt its unusual name.

Instructions

Step 1. Cut the border strips from the white fabric before cutting the pieces for the blocks. First, cut off a little more than 2 1/2 yards, or 94"; trim off the selvage edge. Cut four strips 4" x 94" (the excess will be trimmed later). Set these strips aside. The remaining white fabric is to be used in the blocks.

Step 2. Cut fabric patches as directed on each piece for one block (whole quilt).

Step 3. To piece one block, referring to Figure 1, sew two A pieces together—one print and one solid; repeat. Sew these joined pairs together, matching center seams. Add the

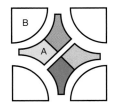

Figure 1
Piece block as shown.

Quilt Measurements
Quilt Size: 79" x 92"   **Block Size:** 6 1/2" x 6 1/2"

Materials
• Scraps for blocks, including floral prints and coordinating solids • 8 yards white fabric for blocks and borders • Backing 83" x 96" • Batting 83" x 96" • 12 yards pink bias binding

curved B pieces to the outside corners to complete one block. Complete 143 blocks to make the quilt as shown. Press blocks.

Step 4. Arrange the blocks in 13 rows of 11 blocks each. Sew the blocks in rows; join the rows to complete the quilt center.

Step 5. Sew the previously cut border strips to the sides of the quilt center. Mark the strips with the scalloped border pattern given in Figure 2 and cut out. (Straight-sided borders may be substituted if you prefer.) Match the fold line on the border pattern with the center of the blocks. Refer to the quilt photograph as needed; press.

Step 6. Sew the remaining borders to the top and bottom in the same manner, mitering corners as instructed on Page 164. Press and trim off excess at backside of corners.

Step 7. Refer to Figure 3 for quilting design used on the sample quilt. Mark design on finished top with a water-erasable marker or pencil.

Step 8. Finish quilt referring to Pages 167–175 for instructions.

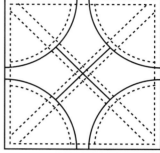

Figure 3
Quilting Design

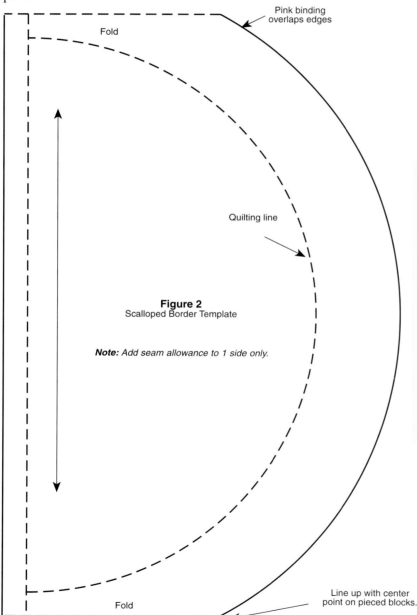

Pink binding overlaps edges

Fold

Quilting line

Figure 2
Scalloped Border Template

Note: Add seam allowance to 1 side only.

Fold

Line up with center point on pieced blocks.

Tips & Techniques

Store templates for a design together in an envelope or plastic see-through jacket. Include a drawing of the pattern or block and templates for each piece marked with the number of pieces needed and the piece number or letter for identification purposes. Just like a puzzle, it is difficult to make a block without a guide, even when you have all the pieces!

Snowball
Placement Diagram
79" x 92"

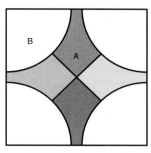

Snowball
6 1/2" x 6 1/2" Block

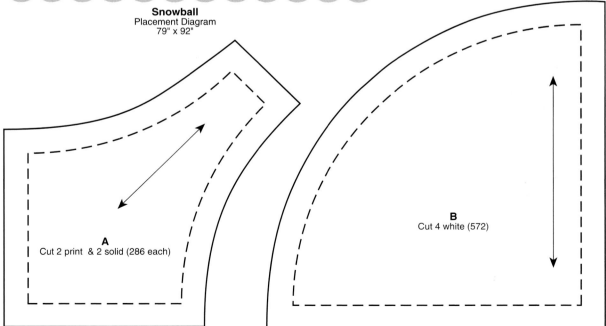

A
Cut 2 print & 2 solid (286 each)

B
Cut 4 white (572)

Grandmother's Choice

The owner of this interesting quilt top purchased it at a yard sale for a mere $20! Along with Davy Crockett hats and Easter bunnies, the fabrics contain flowers, plaids, checks, hearts, paisleys and penguins. Combined, they make a pretty quilt—a great way to unite an odd assortment of scraps.

Search through your collection of scraps to match the creativity of the grandmother who stitched this quilt and you're sure to be pleased with the result. This quilt top is a wonderful example of a block-to-block setting. Notice how the D pieces meet to create a dominant design.

Instructions

Step 1. To complete one block, sew A and AR to long sides of B. Repeat three times. Sew these combined units to C referring to Figure 1. Join sections together to make the center of the block. Add D to outside corners to finish; press.

Figure 1
Piece block in units as shown.

Step 2. Complete 48 blocks to make the quilt as shown. Note that 24 of the blocks show A

Quilt Measurements	
Quilt Size: 72" x 96"	**Block Size:** 12" x 12"

Materials

- 1 1/2 yards blue
- 1 1/2 yards pink
- 5 1/2 yards white
- 5 yards assorted scraps
- 2/3 yard red-and-white check
- Backing 76" x 98"
- Batting 76" x 98"
- 9 1/2 yards purchased or self-made binding

and AR in pink and 24 in blue. These blocks are alternated in the rows.

Step 3. When 48 blocks are complete, assemble the quilt top in eight rows of six blocks each; join the rows as shown in the Placement Diagram. Borders may be added to make a larger quilt.

Step 4. Choose a quilting design or design one of your own. Mark the design on the top referring to the instructions given on Page 165.

Step 5. Finish quilt referring to Pages 167–175 for instructions.

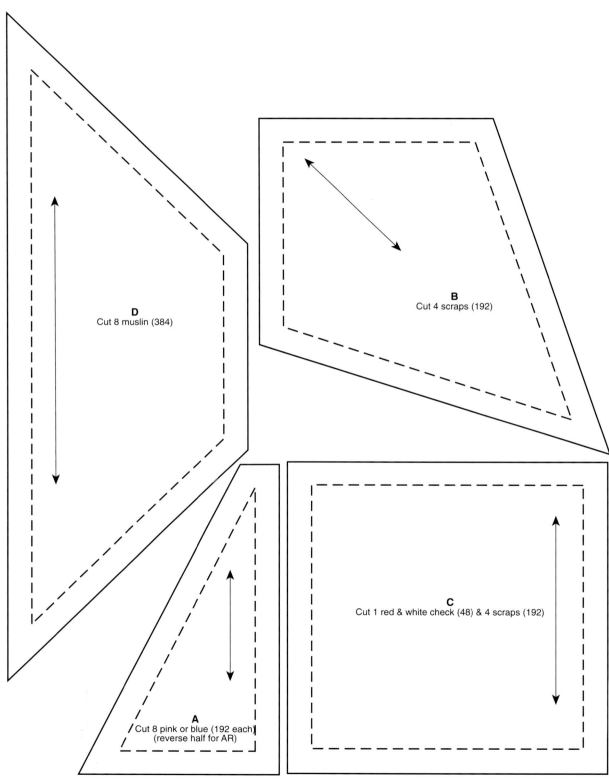

D
Cut 8 muslin (384)

B
Cut 4 scraps (192)

C
Cut 1 red & white check (48) & 4 scraps (192)

A
Cut 8 pink or blue (192 each)
(reverse half for AR)

Grandmother's Choice
12" x 12" Block

Grandmother's Choice
Placement Diagram
72" x 96"

Tips & Techniques

Knots should not show on the quilt top or back. Learn to sink the knot into the batting at the beginning and ending of the quilting thread for successful stitches.

Making 12–18 stitches per inch is a nice goal, but a more realistic goal is 7–9 stitches per inch. Strive for even stitches all the same size that look as good on the back as on the front.

Sunshine & Shadow

This fabulous quilt, also pictured on our cover, is a variation of the Trip Around the World. The difference between the two is only in the placement of the colors that create the pattern.
As you become a more experienced quilter, you'll want to work with color and try creative variations of your favorite quilt patterns.

In the *Sunshine & Shadow* design, fabric squares of the same color run on the diagonal of the quilt. This color may be repeated in subsequent rows, or every row may be different. In the quilt shown, the colors are repeated but with no regular sequence. For the *Trip Around the World* design, the colors make squares around the center, sort of like taking a trip around the world.

Instructions

Step 1. Cut fabric patches as directed in Figure 1 or see instructions in sidebar.

Step 2. Arrange the fabric patches in rows referring to the Placement Diagram.

Step 3. Join the patches in rows or in sections as desired. Press seams of adjoining rows in opposite directions so when rows are joined, seams will lie opposite one another as shown in Figure 2.

Step 4. Join the rows, matching seams as

Quilt Measurements
Quilt Size: Approximately 60 3/4" x 68 1/4"
Template Size: 1 1/4" x 1 1/4"

Materials
• 1/8–1/4 yard each 11 light prints • 1/4 yard each pink, purple, green, blue, aqua and beige solids • 1/3 yard gold solid • 4 yards muslin • Backing 65" x 73" • Batting 65" x 73" • Crochet cotton for tying

shown in Figure 3, being careful to keep the diagonal color design. Press the completed top.

Step 5. Cut border pieces as directed on templates. Sew B to A to B as shown in Figure 4. Complete 34 B-A-B units for each side border strip and 37 for each top and bottom strip.

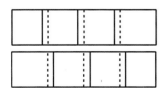

Figure 2
Press seams on rows as shown.

Figure 3
Match seams with seam allowances pressed in opposite directions as shown.

Figure 4
Sew B to A to B as shown.

Step 6. Join the B-A-B units to make strips as in as shown in Figure 5. Press seams in one direction.

Note: *An exact number of A pieces may not fit on border strips. Trim off excess or add more squares and triangles as necessary to make border strips fit. When sewing so many small pieces together, it is difficult to get exact results. No small triangle template is given for ends. Cut strip square to fit.*

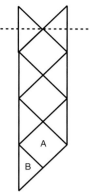

Figure 5
Join the B-A-B units in strips as shown.

Step 7. Cut four muslin strips 2" x 61". Sew a strip to each side of the shorter B-A-B strips as shown in Figure 6. Press seams toward muslin strips. Sew a strip to the two longer sides. Press seams toward border strips. ***Note:*** *Any excess length on the border strips may be trimmed even with the quilt top at this time.*

Figure 6
Add muslin strips to each side of B-A-B strips as shown.

Step 8. Cut four muslin strips 2" x 65 1/2". Sew a strip to each side of the remaining B-A-B strips as before. Sew these strips to the top and

Tips & Techniques

Although the quilt shown was hand-pieced in rows, you might prefer to try cutting strips to construct isolated sections instead of rows as shown in Figure 7. Spend the extra time during the planning stages to save time later. To make a successful Sunshine & Shadow quilt remember these tips:

• Draw the quilt design on graph paper and color it in with colored pencils or markers closely resembling the colors in your fabrics.

• Choose fabrics from your collection and add to them with new purchases.

• Try making a paste-up version of the finished top using tiny fabric squares.

• Find unit repeats on your colored graph by first drawing four-block sections on the graph-paper drawing.

• Look for repeats and determine if they can be made larger.

• Figure out how many of each repeat are needed and how many of each fabric block are needed in each one.

• Can you cut and join strips instead of individual patches to create the repeated sections?

• If so, determine how many squares you can get from a strip and how many strips of each color are needed to complete the quilt.

• Arrange the strips to construct the units, sew together and cut apart to rearrange and sew into units.

• Arrange the units in rows and check to see how the pattern is working.

• When all units are constructed, cut any needed pieces to fill in the design and sew together to complete the top.

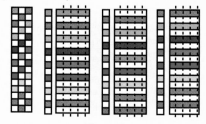

Figure 7
Isolate a section to make strip-pieced units as shown.

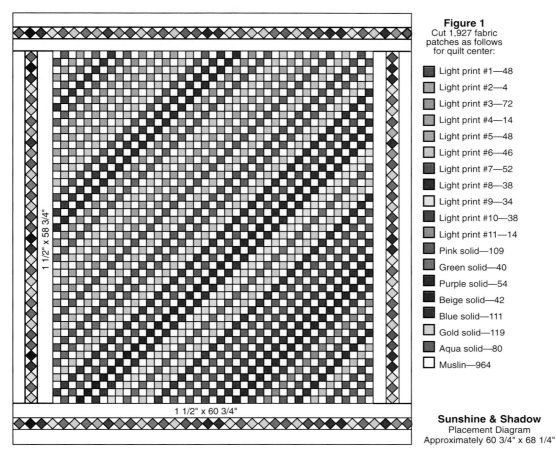

Figure 1
Cut 1,927 fabric
patches as follows
for quilt center:

■ Light print #1—48
■ Light print #2—4
■ Light print #3—72
■ Light print #4—14
■ Light print #5—48
■ Light print #6—46
■ Light print #7—52
■ Light print #8—38
□ Light print #9—34
■ Light print #10—38
■ Light print #11—14
■ Pink solid—109
■ Green solid—40
■ Purple solid—54
■ Beige solid—42
■ Blue solid—111
□ Gold solid—119
■ Aqua solid—80
□ Muslin—964

Sunshine & Shadow
Placement Diagram
Approximately 60 3/4" x 68 1/4"

1 1/2" x 58 3/4"

1 1/2" x 60 3/4"

bottom of the completed top. Press seams toward borders; trim excess.

Step 9. Layer the batting on top of the wrong side of the prepared backing piece. Place the completed top right side down on the batting. Pin layers together with safety pins to hold flat referring to Page 168.

Step 10. Starting in the center of one side, sew all around the top to within 12" of beginning seam. Backstitch to secure seam at the beginning and the end.

Step 11. Turn quilt right side out through the opening. Slipstitch the opening closed by hand. Press quilt edges. Topstitch by machine 1/8" in all around outside edge.

Step 12. Tie quilt on every second or third diagonal row. Refer to Pages 167–175 to finish.

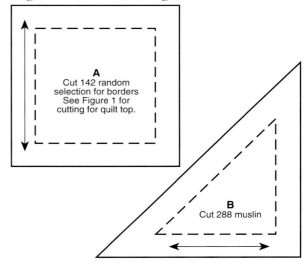

A
Cut 142 random
selection for borders
See Figure 1 for
cutting for quilt top.

B
Cut 288 muslin

Kaleidoscope Variation

*This warm, cheerful antique quilt was made from a variation
of the Kaleidoscope pattern. Although the fabrics date from the last half
of the 19th century, they are still bright and unfaded,
and the quilt itself is in excellent condition.*

The fabrics used in the blocks include white shirtings; red, yellow and blue calicos; and black mourning prints. The blocks were sewn by hand from new scraps and a few heavy fabrics that were cut from previously worn clothing. They all combine to form a splendid quilt.

Instructions

Step 1. To piece one block, arrange the cut pieces for each block on your work surface to form the pattern. Sew light A's to dark #1 A's. Join two A-A units twice; join together in groups of four; join these halves to complete the center circle referring to Figure 1.

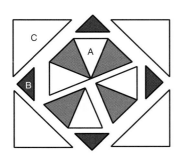

Figure 1
Piece block in units as shown.

Step 2. Sew dark #2 B's to light A's to form the outside corners of the block. Add C to each side to complete the block. Press. Complete 28 blocks.

Quilt Measurements

Quilt Size: 64 1/2" x 68"
Block Size: 8 1/2" x 8 1/2"

Materials

- 2 1/2 yards assorted light fabrics for A and C
- 2 yards dark #1 for A (The quilt shown contains red, yellow and blue prints.)
- 1 yard dark #2 or black
- 2 yards pink
- Backing 68" x 72"
- Batting 68" x 72"
- 8 yards self-made or purchased binding

Step 3. Cut two strips 3" x 68 1/2" from pink and set aside for borders. From the remaining pink fabric, cut 28 squares 9" x 9".

Step 4. Alternate rows with pink squares and pieced blocks to form seven rows each containing four pieced and four pink blocks per row (begin four rows with a pieced block and four rows with a plain block). Sew the blocks into rows and join the rows to complete the top. Press.

Step 5. Sew the 3" pink strips to the top and bottom of the quilt top. Press and trim away any excess fabric.

Step 6. Choose a quilting design or design one of your own. Mark the design on the top referring to the instructions given on Page 165.

Step 7. Finish quilt referring to Pages 167–175 for instructions.

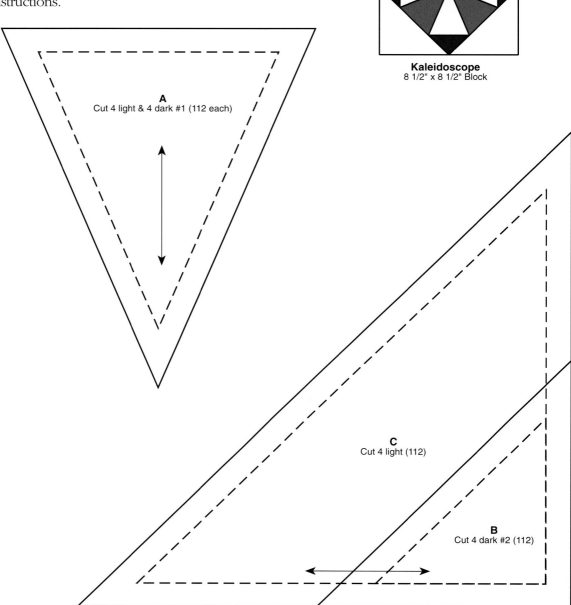

Kaleidoscope
8 1/2" x 8 1/2" Block

A
Cut 4 light & 4 dark #1 (112 each)

C
Cut 4 light (112)

B
Cut 4 dark #2 (112)

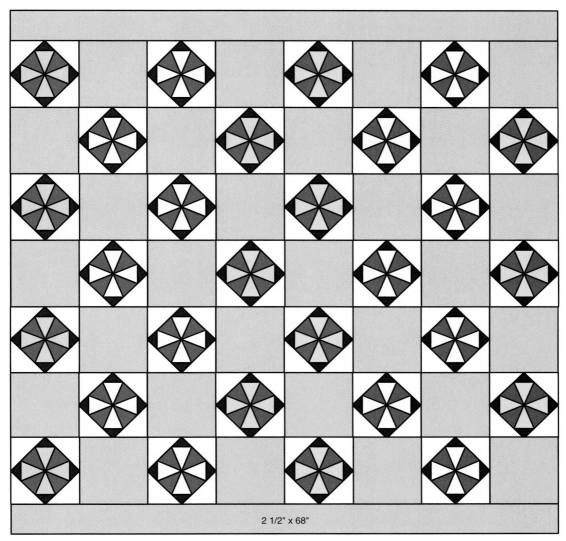

2 1/2" x 68"

Kaleidoscope
Placement Diagram
64 1/2" x 68"

Tips & Techniques

Before machine-piecing fabric patches together, test your sewing machine for positioning an accurate 1/4" seam allowance. There are several tools to help guarantee this. Some machine needles may be moved to allow the presser foot edge to be a 1/4" guide.

A special foot may be purchased for your machine that will guarantee an accurate 1/4" seam. A piece of masking tape can be placed on the throat plate of your sewing machine to mark the 1/4" seam. A plastic stick-on ruler may be used instead of tape.

Rose Dream Quilt

Ann Swengel's grandmother left her a shoe box full of quilting patterns and templates along with this beautiful quilt. Even as we treasure the gifts passed on to us by our grandmothers, so will our children treasure the gifts we give to them. The gift of a quilt expresses the creativity and handiwork of the quilter, a true gift from the soul.

Curved seams are a bit more difficult to piece. Begin by pinning matching pieces together at beginning and ending seam joints. Ease the shapes together, pinning at close intervals to allow the convex shape to fit into the concave shape.

Accomplishing curved seams with hand-piecing is easier than by machine-piecing, but it is possible for an experienced sewer to successfully seam curved pieces by machine.

Instructions

Note: The quilt shown contains blocks made with several shades of blue and yellow mixed with several other prints. If you prefer a more planned quilt, purchase fabrics of several colors and arrange in rows as desired.

Step 1. Cut fabric pieces for each block as directed on templates.

Step 2. To piece one block, add two A pieces to C. To the remaining C, add B and set into the curve of the A-C-A unit. Repeat this four times for each block referring to Figure 1. Join the four units to complete the block. Repeat for 20 blocks and arrange as shown in the Placement Diagram or as desired.

Step 3. For borders, cut two pieces 6 1/2" x 52 1/2" for top and bottom and two pieces

Quilt Measurements

Quilt Size: 64" x 77"   **Block Size:** 13" x 13"

Materials

- 3 yards white background fabric
- 2 1/2 yards border fabric
- Scraps 12" x 12" for each block
- Batting 67" x 80"
- Backing 67" x 80"

6 1/2" x 77 1/2" for long sides. Add to quilt top as shown in the Placement Diagram.

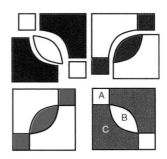

Figure 1
Complete 4 units as shown to make 1 block.

Step 4. The quilting design used in the blocks is in sets of squares, similar to concentric circles around each other. The center square is arranged as a diamond over the place where the middle edge of one block meets another. Mark the border quilting pattern given referring to Figure 2. Mark the remainder of the quilt top and prepare for quilting referring to Pages 163–170.

Step 5. When quilting is complete, trim the back and batting 1" smaller than the top all

Figure 2
Mark the border quilting design as shown.

around. Turn the top edge under and to the back to finish.

Putting It All Together

Constructing a top is only part of the task involved in completing a quilt. Finishing that top into a completed quilt for use includes several skills. Our grandmothers often hand-quilted or tied their quilts; machine quilting was not a common method used during those times. Quiltmakers today have many books and expert teachers from which to learn helpful techniques for hand or machine quilting.

Many steps are required to prepare a quilt top for quilting, including setting the blocks together, adding borders, choosing and marking quilting designs, layering the top, batting and backing for quilting, the quilting or tying process and finishing the edges of the quilt.

It is no wonder that many of our grand-mothers never finished their tops as evidenced by a few beautiful unfinished tops shown in this book. Why would Grandmother spend so much time completing a top which would never be finished? Could she have intentionally spent time

on sewing something just because she loved to do it? Did she sometimes feel just a little guilty like we do when we don't finish everything we start?

As you begin the process of finishing your quilt top, strive for a neat, flat quilt with square sides and corners, not for perfection—that will come with time. Your work will get better with practice, and practice comes with making more quilts!

• Try several different methods to find the one that works best for you.

• Document your time and expenses by keeping a journal for each quilt.

• Make one sample of each block design; combine these sample blocks to make a sampler quilt.

• Sampler quilts are fun because each block is different, which means you learn something new with each one.

• Copy the pattern diagram several times and try different color combinations.

Rose Dream Quilt
Placement Diagram
64" x 77"

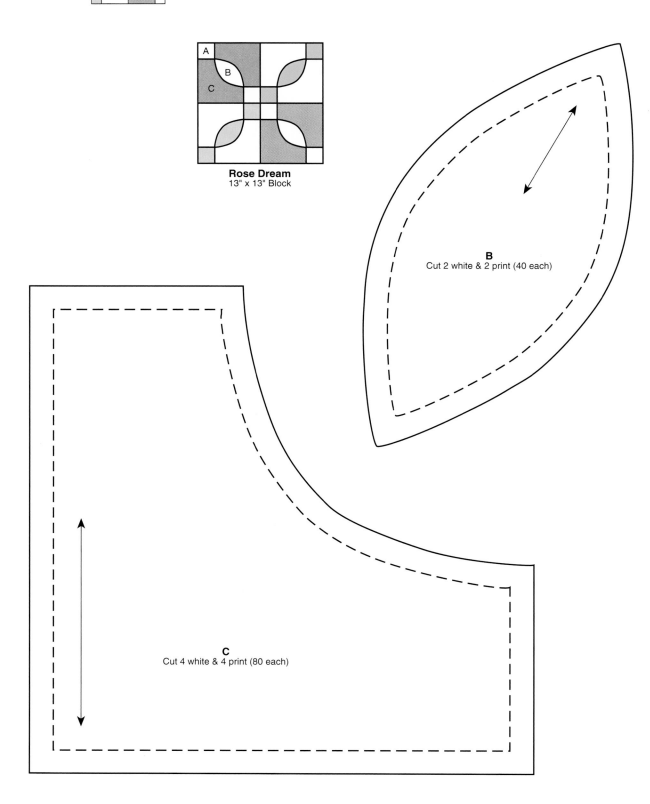

Rose Dream
13" x 13" Block

B
Cut 2 white & 2 print (40 each)

C
Cut 4 white & 4 print (80 each)

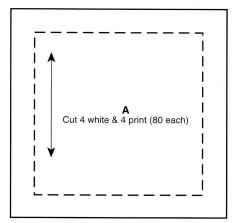

A
Cut 4 white & 4 print (80 each)

Tips & Techniques

If border fabrics are also used in the quilt top, cut border strips the required width and several inches longer than needed before cutting fabric patches for blocks or units. This guarantees border strips won't require piecing.

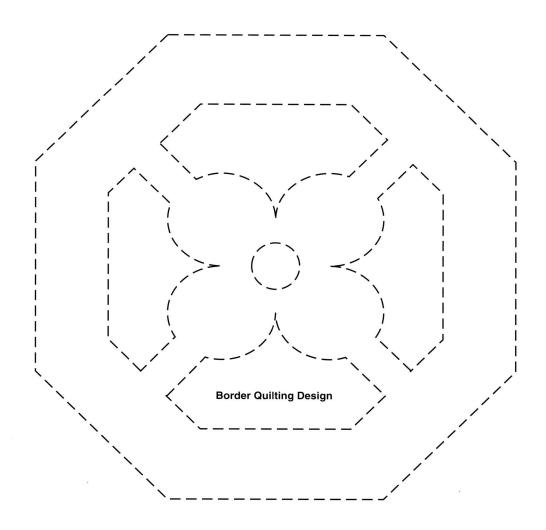

Border Quilting Design

Unit Piecing

Unit piecing can be very satisfying. The small pieces are easily portable, and units can be stitched a few at a time.

These popular old-time quilt designs are made up of pieced units joined by connecting pieces that cannot be assembled in the traditional block format.

Sometimes there are no connecting pieces, and only a change in color indicates the change in unit. This type of quilt is best worked on when time permits.

You'll enjoy making unit quilts a little at a time!

Tips & Techniques for

Unit Piecing

Unit piecing can be one of the most beautiful quilt patterns, and it was always a favorite of our grandmothers. The quilts shown in this section are most often hand-pieced, although experienced machine stitchers might find it possible to complete the quilts by machine.

The templates must usually be cut individually, instead of rotary-cut. Trying to work continuously until all units are finished can sometimes seem to take a long time. However, the results are well worth the effort.

Fabric. The scraps for a unit-pieced quilt can be gathered a small amount at a time. Unit-pieced quilts make great projects for scrap exchanges.

• Cut pieces for unit quilts a little at a time. Cutting them all at once is a big job, and no fun at all!

• Purchase the background fabric all at once so that all the connecting pieces will be the same.

Take-Along Kits. This type of quilt is best saved to be worked on a little at a time when time permits.

• Make traveling kits so you'll always have something ready to take with you to work on while waiting for appointments or for children at games and practices, or even while riding in the car.

• Ideas for portable containers include zippered bank bags, jewelry bags and plastic storage containers.

Scissors and Shears. Beautiful scissors were found in the sewing baskets of days gone by. Attention to beauty in such a functional item was not uncommon. Beautiful scissors are available today as well, but remember that the functional scissors or shears cut fabric with little or no resistance—beauty has nothing to do with function. Good, sharp scissors and shears are mandatory.

• Scissors handles are not bent and have two handle holes that are the same size. Generally scissors are used for trimming small areas and cutting threads.

• Shears have a smaller hole for thumb placement, a large hole for several fingers, and bent handles to allow them to slide easily while cutting along a flat surface. Shears are used for large cutting jobs such as cutting patchwork pieces.

• Paper-cutting scissors are a must for cutting templates out of cardboard and plastic. They, too, must be sharp and sturdy.

Thimbles. Hand quilters find thimbles very useful. They save wear and tear on fingers and help you make quilting stitches go all the way through all layers of the fabric.

• Getting accustomed to using a thimble may seem difficult at first; persevere and you will find you won't be able to sew without one.

• Thimbles are available in gold, silver, metal, plastic, leather, glass, and wood.

• Experiment with some of the new versions of thimbles that will fit any finger on your hand.

Be sure to read General Instructions for Quiltmaking, beginning on Page 152, before you begin your project.

Grandmother's Flower Garden

The Grandmother's Flower Garden was one of Grandmother's most popular patterns. The quilt shown is similar to many quilts of this design from those early days. This scrap quilt has worn edges, but is softer and just as warm as the day it was finished over 50 years ago.

The flowers in this quilt are made with three rounds of hexagons all with the same color center. The flowers are separated with a row of muslin hexagons and small green triangles. The triangles could have been eliminated and the hexagon shapes stitched to one another, but the green triangles and muslin hexagons create a walkway, or path, in the garden of flowers.

Instructions

Step 1. Cut fabric patches for one hexagon flower referring to Figure 1. Beginning with the first row, sew a solid-color A to each side of the center A, joining as shown in Figure 2. Add a round of print A's and then a round of muslin A's to complete one flower unit.

Step 2. Piece 102 flower units.

Step 3. Join nine flower units with solid green

Quilt Measurements
Quilt Size: Approximately 74 1/4" x 88 1/2" **Unit Size:** 8 1/4" x 9 1/4"

Materials
• 4 yards muslin • 1 3/4 yards green solid • 1 yard gold solid • 1/8–1/4 yard each variety of solids and prints for flower petals • Backing 78" x 92" • Batting 78" x 92" • 20 yards self-made or purchased binding

B diamonds and C triangles to make a row referring to Figure 3. Repeat for six rows.

Figure 1
Arrange hexagons for 1 unit as shown.

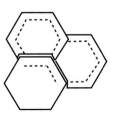

Figure 2
Sew hexagon shapes to one another as shown.

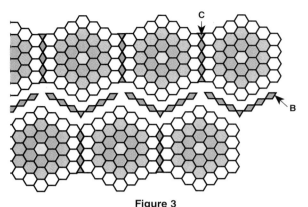

Figure 3
Join flower units with green solid B diamonds
and C triangles in rows.

Step 4. Complete 10 half-flower shapes as shown in Figure 4. Join two half-units with eight pieced flower units to make five rows, beginning and ending with half-units.

Figure 4
Make half-flowers as shown.

Step 5. Join eight whole flower units to make one row for the top.

Step 6. Join the rows with B diamonds and C triangles referring to the Placement Diagram and Figure 3 again to complete the quilt top.

Step 7. Prepare the pieced top for quilting.

Note: *The quilt shown was quilted 1/4" from seams on all hexagons. This is the most common way to quilt the pattern.*

Step 8. Finish quilt as desired referring to Pages 167–175.

Note: *The quilt shown was bound around each hexagon shape on the edge. It was not squared off. This edge finish looks very nice and,*

although it takes more time than a straight-edge finish, adding pieces to square up the edge would add time to the completion of the quilt top. A double binding would be more durable. The edges on the antique quilt shown are very worn and need to be rebound.

Tips & Techniques

English paper piecing was sometimes used to sew hexagon units together to complete the flowers for the Grandmother's Flower Garden design. There are many ways to color the flowers to make different designs as shown in Figures 5 and 6. Removing the B diamonds and C triangles gives the design a little different look once it is finished. Whether or not you have a green thumb, this flower garden can be beautiful now and every season of the year with very little care.

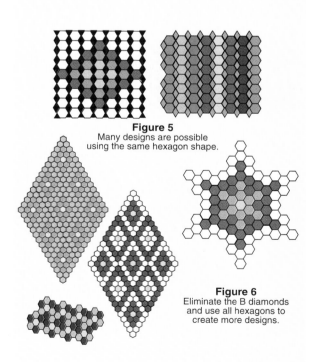

Figure 5
Many designs are possible
using the same hexagon shape.

Figure 6
Eliminate the B diamonds
and use all hexagons to
create more designs.

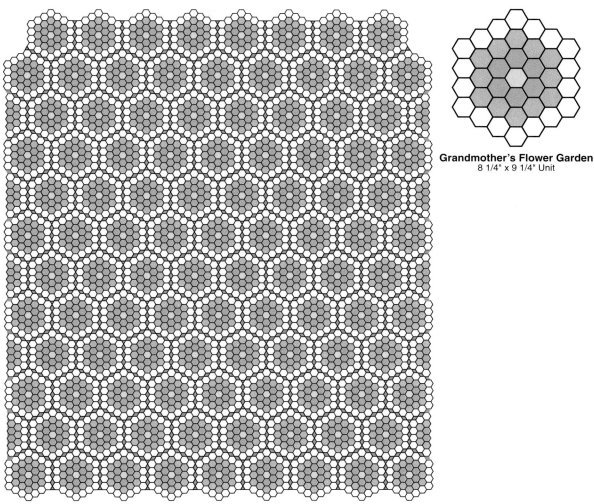

Grandmother's Flower Garden
8 1/4" x 9 1/4" Unit

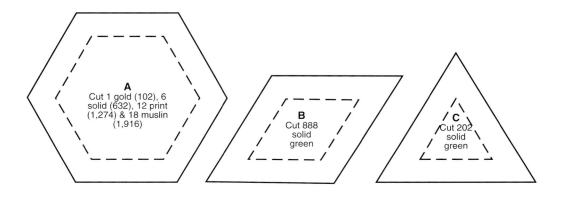

Grandmother's Flower Garden
Placement Diagram
Approximately 74 1/4" x 88 1/2"

A
Cut 1 gold (102), 6
solid (632), 12 print
(1,274) & 18 muslin
(1,916)

B
Cut 888
solid
green

C
Cut 202
solid
green

Connecting Star

A perfect example of a unit-pieced quilt, the Connecting Star units are joined with orange solid diamonds. You may not prefer the colorful fabric of the antique quilt shown. However, in Grandmother's day, orange was a popular color. Combined with the green solid of the day, you may be surprised how much you like this fascinating color combination.

Regardless of whether you choose the colors Grandmother used or connect your star shapes with a country blue or rose, you will enjoy piecing the star units while using up scraps from your accumulated stash.

Instructions

Step 1. Cut four strips orange solid 2" x 70" and four strips 2" x 74" before cutting templates. Set aside. Cut two strips green solid 2" x 70" and two strips 2" x 74". Set aside.

Note: *These strips are at least 2" longer than needed to finish the quilt as is to allow for adjustments when sewing. The excess is trimmed after the corners are mitered.*

Step 2. Cut four A pieces per unit—two light prints and 2 dark prints. Join a light print to a dark print twice. Join the two pieced sections to create one star unit referring to Figure 1.

Figure 1
Join A pieces to make 1 star unit as shown.

Step 3. Complete 182 star units. Arrange in 14 rows of 13 units each. When you have found a pleasing arrangement, pin units in rows in order. Begin joining rows with B pieces

Quilt Measurements
Quilt Size: 67 1/2" x 72"
Unit Size: 4 1/2" x 4 1/2"

Materials
• 4 yards orange solid
• 2 yards green solid
• Assorted dark and light print scraps to total 2 1/2 yards
• Backing 72" x 76"
• Batting 72" x 76"
• 8 1/2 yards self-made or purchased binding

between referring to Figure 2, starting and ending each row with C as shown in Figure 3.

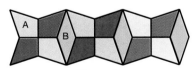

Figure 2
Set star units together with B as shown.

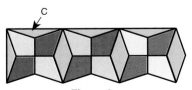

Figure 3
On edge pieces, use C as shown.

Step 4. Join the rows with B pieces, with C on the edge of the top and bottom rows, referring to Figure 4.

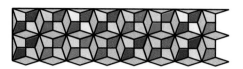

Figure 4
Join the rows with B using C on the top, bottom and side rows.

Step 5. Sew a 2" x 70" orange strip to each side of a 2" x 70" green strip; repeat. Press seams to one side.

Step 6. Sew a 2" x 74" orange strip to each side of a 2" x 74" green strip; repeat. Press seams to one side.

Step 7. Sew the longer strips to the long sides of the quilt top and the shorter strips to the short sides, mitering corners referring to Page

165. Press seams toward border strips. Trim off excess from backside of corners. Press completed quilt top.

Step 8. Finish quilt as desired referring to Pages 167–175.

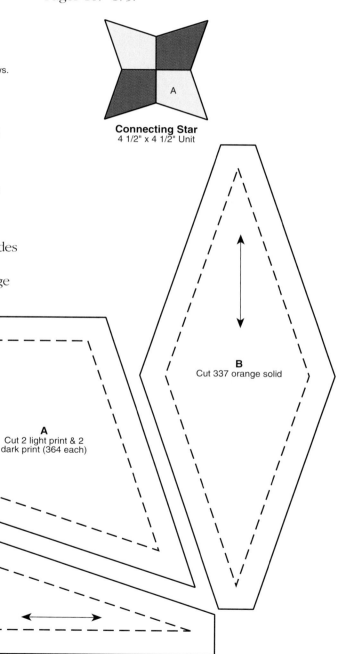

Connecting Star
4 1/2" x 4 1/2" Unit

A

B
Cut 337 orange solid

A
Cut 2 light print & 2
dark print (364 each)

C
Cut 54
orange
solid

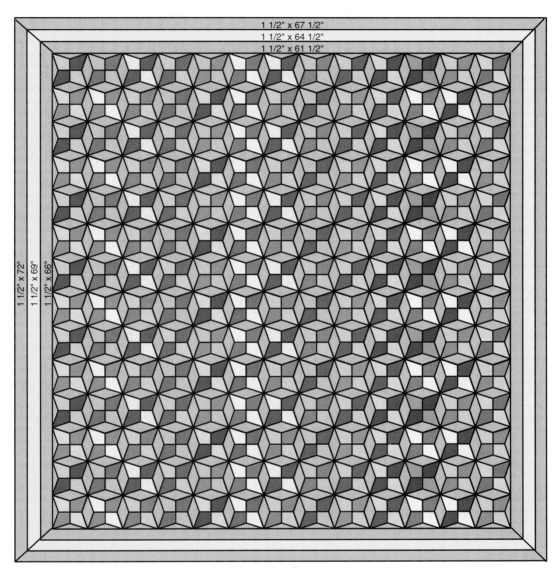

Connecting Star
Placement Diagram
67 1/2" x 72"

Tips & Techniques

It is best to use the same method of adding borders throughout. If your quilt will be judged, one of the criteria judges look for is consistency in design. Borders with butted corners combined with borders with mitered corners don't always work.

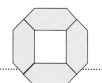

Old-Fashioned Quilt

Many quilts could be called old-fashioned, but the name of the quilt pattern shown is really Old-Fashioned Quilt. The pattern was sent to the Kansas City Star by Mrs. Karl Harms from Ionia, Missouri, in 1937. The quilt shown is a perfect example of this all-over design made with only two fabrics, the yellow being very typical of that used in the '30s.

By introducing more than two colors to this longtime favorite pattern, you will completely change the look of the quilt. Before you begin, experiment with colored pencils and photocopies of the Placement Diagram. You'll enjoy discovering creative ways to use some of your treasured fabric scraps.

Instructions

Step 1. Piece units by sewing A to B as shown in Figure 1. Complete row units making two types of rows referring to Figure 2. You will need nine rows of 14 B squares and eight half-unit rows. Each crosswise row has 14 B pieces and each lengthwise row has 17 B pieces.

Quilt Measurements
Quilt Size: 72" x 87"   **Unit Size:** 7" x 7"

Materials
• 2 yards solid white • 5 1/4 yards yellow print • Backing 74" x 89" • Batting 74" x 89" • 11 yards self-made or purchased binding

Figure 1
Sew A to B as shown.

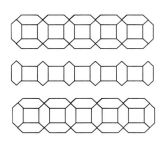

Figure 2
Join pieces to make rows instead of blocks as shown. Join whole-unit rows with half-unit rows as shown.

Step 2. Arrange completed rows in sequence and join together to complete pieced top. Press.

Step 3. Mark chosen quilting design on B squares using a water-erasable marker or pencil. The design used on the quilt shown is marked in dotted lines on B. The A pieces are quilted 1/4" and 1/2" in from seams on each piece.

Step 4. Finish quilt referring to Pages 167–175 for instructions.

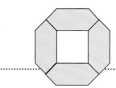

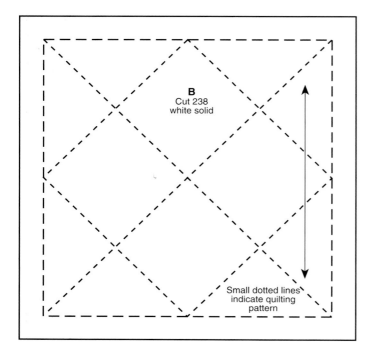

B
Cut 238
white solid

Small dotted lines
indicate quilting
pattern

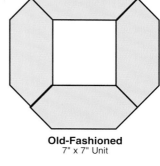

Old-Fashioned
7" x 7" Unit

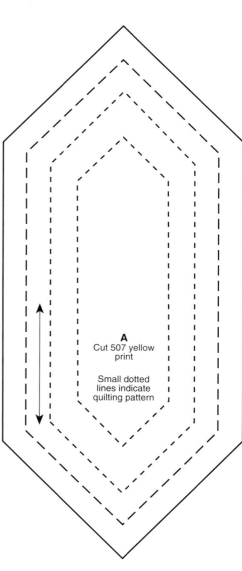

A
Cut 507 yellow
print

Small dotted
lines indicate
quilting pattern

Tips & Techniques

Hand-sewing needles can be purchased in packages with all one size or in a variety of sizes. Needles are numbered 1 through 12 and categorized as sharps or betweens. Sharps are all-purpose needles which can be used for appliqué and patchwork piecing. Betweens are used for quilting. The higher the number, the finer and shorter the needle. The recommended size range is 7–12 for quiltmaking.

The size of the sewing machine needle to use is determined by the fabrics and threads and the type of stitch you are using. Your sewing machine's manual makes good suggestions for this. As a general rule, a size #80/12 needle is used for everyday sewing. A #90/14 is used for heavier fabrics and threads. Remember, when you are machine-quilting, the many layers require a larger needle (at least #90/14). Special machine-quilting needles may be purchased as well.

Old-Fashioned Quilt
Placement Diagram
72" x 87"

Lone Star

This marvelous quilt was recovered from the trunk of a car where it was used as a liner! It has also been used as a table cover and a wall hanging, and has been hung over a cabinet door to add color to a room. Oh, the fascinating stories a quilt could tell!

The *Lone Star* design is made using only one diamond-shaped template. Whether made with a planned color scheme as the quilt shown, or with scraps, the resulting quilt is always beautiful. Careful, creative color selection is the key to designing this striking star quilt.

Instructions

Step 1. Prepare a template using the A diamond shape given.

Step 2. Cut the number of pieces specified on the template for each color.

Step 3. Arrange the pieces in stacked rows in the shape of the star point. Join patches together in rows, referring to Figure 1.

Note: *You might prefer to piece one star point at a time, or to piece the same row for each point all at once.*

Quilt Measurements
Quilt Size: 77" x 85"
Block Size: 22 1/2" x 22 1/2"

Materials
• 5 yards white for diamonds and background squares and triangles
• 1 1/4 yards red solid
• 1 1/2 yards gold solid
• Backing 81" x 89"
• Batting 81" x 89"
• 10 yards self-made or purchased binding

Step 4. When the rows are stitched, join to make star points referring to Figure 1. You will need eight points with nine rows in each point.

Step 5. Join the star-point units starting in the center. Join four points; press and set aside. Join remaining four points; press. Sew the two halves together to finish star section.

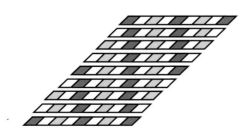

Figure 1
Assemble star points in rows as shown.

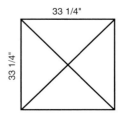

Figure 2
Cut side fill-in triangles as shown.

Step 6. Cut four squares white 23" x 23" for corners. Cut one square white 33 1/4" x 33 1/4". Cut in half on the diagonal twice to make side fill-in triangles referring to Figure 2.

Note: Due to different sewing techniques, your star points may be a different size. Measure the distance from one intersecting point to the outside point, measuring to the exact spot where they will intersect (not including seam allowance on star points). Write the measurement down. Do the same to several other sides. Each measurement should be the same. This is the size of the square needed to complete your top. Add a 1/4" seam allowance all around and this is the size square you will need. Cut four of these squares and set into points. The fill-in triangles are measured in the same way. Remember to add a seam allowance on all three sides before cutting. Be sure to place the long edge of the triangle on the straight of grain to reduce stretching on the outside edge of your quilt.

Step 7. Piece four star blocks referring to Figure 3. Fold the white squares in half both vertically and horizontally and crease to mark centers. Place a pieced star shape on each background block, using crease marks as guides for placement. Turn under edges of pieced star shapes and appliqué in place using matching thread.

Figure 3
Piece 4 star blocks for corners as shown.

Step 8. Set the squares into the corners and the triangles in between points on the sides; press.

Step 9. Cut two border strips 4 1/2" x 77 1/2"; add to the top and bottom; press. **Note:** *These borders were only added to two sides, probably to make the quilt longer to fit on a bed. More borders may be added to make a quilt of larger size.*

Step 10. Choose a quilting design for the squares and fill-in triangles. The antique quilt shown was quilted in straight lines all over. Mark and prepare quilt top for quilting referring to Page 167.

Step 11. Finish quilt referring to Pages 167–175.

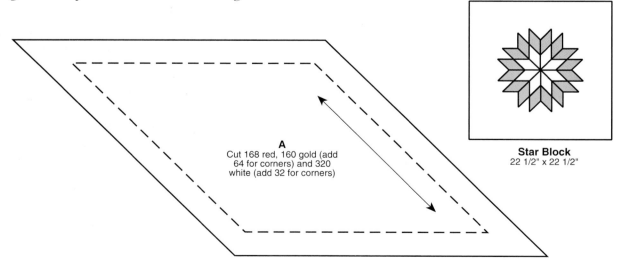

A
Cut 168 red, 160 gold (add 64 for corners) and 320 white (add 32 for corners)

Star Block
22 1/2" x 22 1/2"

4" x 77"

Lone Star
Placement Diagram
77" x 85"

Hexagon Snowflake

*Some things in life require dedication and persistence. So it is with quilting.
Don't let the challenge of thousands of tiny pieces keep you from
making this colorful masterpiece. A skillful grandmother
obviously spent many hours stitching this gorgeous work of art.*

This hand-pieced top has more than 4,100 pieces! The B piece is so small, it is barely big enough to see. An expert may be able to machine-piece the units, but hand-piecing is recommended. Piece the top in units and join the units in vertical rows. Half-units are used at the top and bottom to square off the quilt. Borders wouldn't be necessary to finish this quit. Quilting in the ditch of the hexagon pieces would be a daunting but worthwhile project.

Instructions

Step 1. Prepare fabric and templates as directed on Pagess 154–156 for hand-piecing.

Step 2. To complete one unit, sew A and B pieces in three sections referring to Figure 1; press.

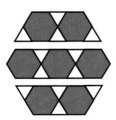

Figure 1
Piece unit in 3 sections.

Step 3. Join the sections to complete one unit; press. Complete 189 units.

Quilt Measurements
Quilt Size: 63" x 73 1/2"
Unit Size: 4 1/2" x 5 1/4"

Materials
• 3 3/4 yards muslin
• 189 scrap pieces 8" square for A pieces in each unit
• Batting 67" x 77"
• Backing 67" x 77"
• 8 yards self-made or purchased binding

Step 4. Join the units in rows of 14 using piece C to connect units referring to Figure 2.

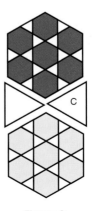

Figure 2
Join units with C in rows as shown.

Add 1/2 C to first and last block in each row. Repeat for seven rows. Join the remaining units in seven rows of 13; press.

Step 5. Sew 14 half-blocks using lines on templates to make half-templates. Piece half-units as shown in Figure 3; press.

Step 6. Add the half-units to each end of the rows with 13 units; press.

Step 7. Join the rows to complete pieced top referring to the Placement Diagram; press.

Step 8. Finish as desired referring to Pages 167–175.

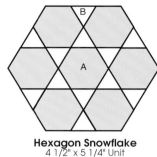

Hexagon Snowflake
4 1/2" x 5 1/4" Unit

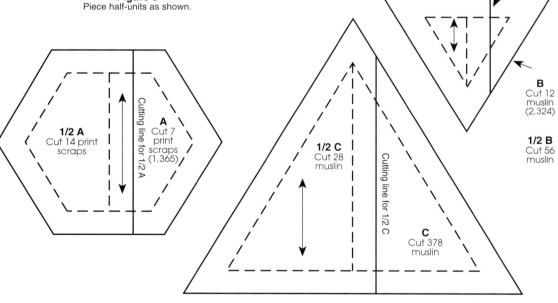

Figure 3
Piece half-units as shown.

Tips & Techniques

A good household iron will do the job for quiltmaking, and there are many brands available with a wide range of prices.

Some commercial and professional irons have a larger water reservoir and a higher capacity for steam than a household iron. They are lightweight and easy to handle.

Some quiltmakers do not recommend using steam for ironing pieces because it can stretch them out of shape.

Hexagon Snowflake
Placement Diagram
63" x 73 1/2"

Double Wedding Ring

The Double Wedding Ring is one of the most popular quilt designs of all time. Its symbolism can't be overlooked. The rings with no beginning or end symbolize the love that is bound together in a wedding. Grandmother made this quilt often as a wedding gift for her children and grandchildren.

Made up of a variety of small scraps combined with pink and green connecting corner and white centers, this quilt is typical of the *Double Wedding Ring* made in the 1930s. The edges are finished in the shape of the block. Bias binding must be used to allow the edge finish to stretch around the curved edges of the design. The green color is the perfect choice to accent this pretty edge.

Instructions

Step 1. Prepare templates referring to Pages 154 and 155. Cut as directed on each piece for one block (whole quilt). Piece one block before cutting all pieces.

Step 2. Join nine A pieces to make a wedge unit as shown in Figure 1. Repeat for eight units. Join two units with D and set on B referring to Figure 2. Repeat for four wedges.

Figure 1
Join 9 A pieces to make 1 wedge unit.

Figure 2
Join 2 wedge units with D and set in B.

Quilt Measurements
Quilt Size: Approximately 63 3/8" x 86 1/2"
Unit Size: 17 1/4" x 17 1/4"

Materials
• Scraps for A pieces
• 1 yard each pink and green solids
• 3 3/4 yards white
• Backing 68" x 91"
• Batting 68" x 91"
• 12 yards self-made or purchased binding

Step 3. Set the four wedges together with C to complete one ring as shown in Figure 3. Piece 12 whole rings.

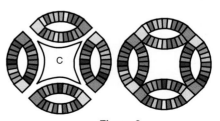

Figure 3
Sew 4 wedges together with C to complete 1 ring.

Step 4. Piece 15 half-rings as shown in Figure 4. Piece four wedge units, referring to Figure 2 again. Arrange three half-rings with two wedges and four C's to make one row referring to Figure 5. Repeat for two rows.

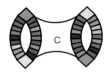

Figure 4
Piece a half-ring as shown.

Step 5. Join the three half-rings with four whole rings to make a row as shown in Figure 6. Repeat for three rows.

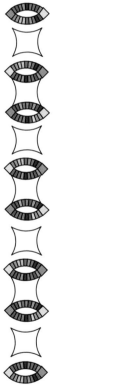

Figure 5
Join 3 half-rings with 2 wedges and 4 C's to make a row as shown.

Figure 6
Join 4 whole rings with 3 half-rings as shown.

Step 6. Join the half-ring rows and the whole-ring rows referring to Figure 7. Set in remaining B pieces between resulting scallops around the

edges referring to the Placement Diagram to complete the quilt top.

Figure 7
Arrange pieced rows as shown.

Step 7. Choose a pretty quilting design for the C piece or mark with crossing diagonal lines as shown on the quilt. Mark chosen design on the quilt top referring to Page 167 for instructions.

Step 8. Finish quilt referring to Pages 167–175 for instructions.

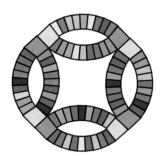

Double Wedding Ring
17 1/4" x 17 1/4" Ring

Double Wedding Ring
Placement Diagram
Approximately 63 3/8" x 86 1/2"

The Double Wedding Ring Quilt

Grandma gave us a Double Wedding Ring *quilt,*

two kisses after wedding vows were whispered.

My groom, an engineer, nor I, could ever figure

by calculus or computer wizardry the numbers

of slanted 1" squares which locked the Wedding

Rings to one another.

A maze of colored snippets pieced together

by aunts, cousins and friends sitting 'round a

wooden frame, squinting to thread small-eyed

needles again and again.

They laughed, joked, imagined newlyweds

snuggling in their double bed.

Each morning over 20 wedded years wife

patted, smoothed and admired the

interwoven rings.

Over time the colors faded, here and there the

stitches loosened lifelong promises worn.

Husband wayward, wife forlorn.

The quilt so patiently sewn, so tenderly cared

for, given to bind two as one, now a forgotten

heirloom at the Smithsonian.

—*By Mildred Toogood*

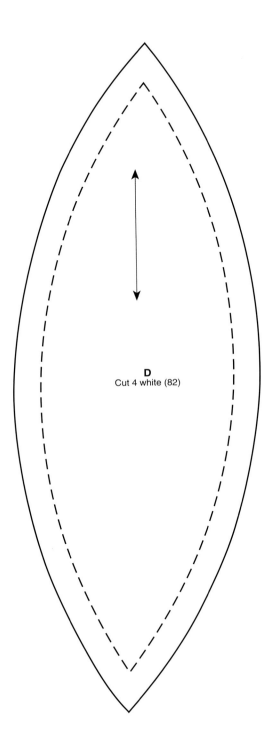

D
Cut 4 white (82)

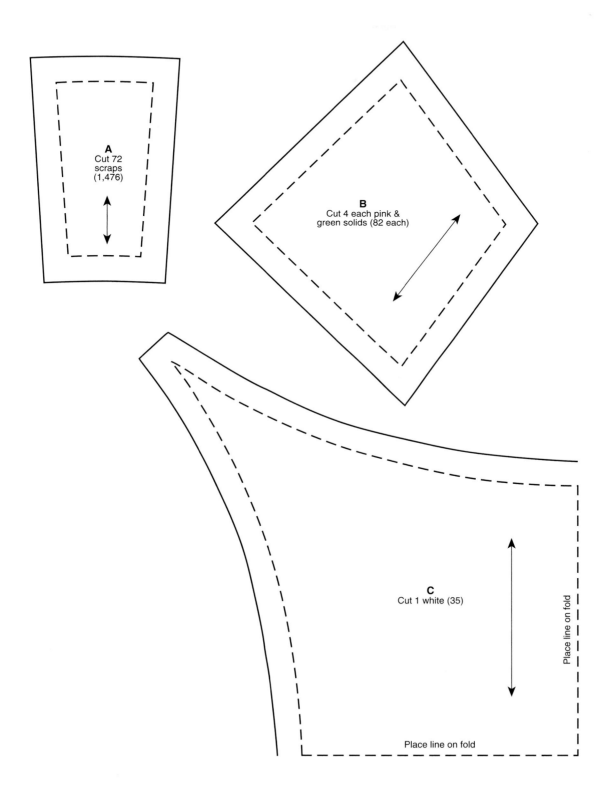

A
Cut 72
scraps
(1,476)

B
Cut 4 each pink &
green solids (82 each)

C
Cut 1 white (35)

Place line on fold

Place line on fold

Appliqué

Our grandmothers liked to appliqué almost as much as they liked to piece.

You need only look at the many wonderful appliquéd quilts from the 1930s to see that the appliqué trend was in vogue.

Favorite patterns from that time such as Sunbonnet Sue, Overall Bill and butterfly designs are still popular today.

Reach into your 1990s scrap bag and pull out fabric patches to create a quilt Grandmother would be proud to claim as her own!

Tips & Techniques for

Appliqué

Although there have always been many more pieced patterns than appliqué patterns to choose from, our grandmothers loved to appliqué. Talk to almost anyone about quilting and she will know exactly what you are referring to when you mention *Sunbonnet Sue.*

In this section of appliqué quilts we share a baby quilt of one of these popular patterns, *Sunbonnet Sue & Overall Bill,* along with *T-Tulips* and *Summer Butterflies.* All are made using colorful fabric from Grandmother's scrap bag. Whether you choose to work by hand or machine, you will be delighted with these lovely appliquéd quilt patterns.

Appliqué Tips. Appliqué is much like painting a picture except that you use different fabric instead of different colors of paint.

• Remember that appliqué patterns are given as full-size designs.

• Make separate templates for each piece, adding a seam allowance when cutting for hand appliqué. Our grandmothers used whatever they could find to make templates. Lightweight cardboard was the most commonly used material, then plastic, when it became widely available. Cardboard templates work well for a time, but after use the edges can get worn and distorted.

• Templates must be accurate in order for all the pieces to fit together nicely. Mark each template with the pattern name and the piece number or letter to identify it.

• Appliqué the designs in numerical order.

• Do not turn under a seam allowance on pieces where another piece overlaps it. This will reduce bulk.

• Remember that the measurements given on the Placement Diagrams are the sizes that the quilt should end up being after stitching *perfect* 1/4" seams. Your stitching may not be exactly perfect so cut border strips longer than necessary and trim to exact size when the center of the quilt top is complete.

Finding the Center of a Block. When working with background blocks, find the center by folding the square vertically, horizontally and diagonally. Crease the folds by hand. The fold lines will be your guide for centering and placing designs.

Embellishments. These little extras make a project special and unique.

• Appliqué designs may be embellished with embroidery, lace and other accents.

• Grandmother may have used black embroidery floss and a buttonhole stitch to appliqué some designs, but you can try other methods.

• You can easily make your quilt any size by varying the number of blocks, by making wider borders or by adding more borders. Don't forget to purchase extra fabric to make these changes, if necessary.

Be sure to read General Instructions for Quiltmaking, beginning on Page 152, for more tips and techniques to help you make a lovely appliquéd quilt.

T-Tulips

A sure sign of warm days to come are the bright, colorful tulips swaying gracefully in the spring air. Our grandmothers must have surely welcomed springtime, when the house could be aired and thoroughly cleaned after a long winter. A lovely tulip quilt such as this one was an ever-present reminder of new beginnings.

This delightful 1930s quilt was purchased at an antique sale in Monroe, Washington, the loving handiwork of an unknown quiltmaker. The vintage green and orange fabrics were widely used in quilts of the Depression era, and this Nancy Cabot *T-Tulips* pattern shows the colors off perfectly. The creative border design is a symbol of row after row of tulips bobbing in the wind.

Instructions

Step 1. Cut 48 muslin squares 8 1/2" x 8 1/2" for background.

Step 2. Prepare background blocks for appliqué by folding in half vertically, horizontally and diagonally, creasing with each fold to mark centers.

Step 3. Matching X marked on pattern to creases on blocks, appliqué pieces in place on background blocks in numerical order using chosen method referring to Pages 159–161.

Step 4. Cut 24 orange squares 5" x 5". Cut each square on the diagonal to make 48 triangles.

Step 5. With right sides together, sew the orange triangle to the corner of the 8 1/2" block as shown in Figure 1. Trim 1/4" from seam through both layers; press the seam to one side.

Quilt Measurements
Quilt Size: Approximately 81" x 100"
Block Size: 8" x 8"

Materials
• Scraps for flowers and scallop border
• 1/2 yard orange
• 3 3/4 yards muslin
• 3 yards green
• Backing 85" x 104"
• Batting 85" x 104"
• 10 1/2 yards self-made or purchased binding

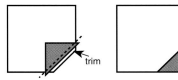

Figure 1
Sew orange triangles to corners of background blocks.

Step 6. Place four appliquéd blocks together with the orange fabric making a square in the center as shown in Figure 2. Repeat for 12 blocks.

Step 7. Cut nine green sashing strips 3 1/2" x 16 1/2" and two strips 3 1/2" x 73 1/2".

Figure 2
Sew 4 blocks together as shown.

short strips to the top and bottom and the long strips to the sides, mitering corners; press.

Step 12. Cut 90 A pieces from floral scraps. Cut 86 B pieces from muslin background.

Step 13. Sew A to B to A to B until you have a strip of 20 A units; repeat. Sew another strip with 25 A units; repeat.

Step 14. Sew the shorter strips to the top and bottom, adjusting to fit. Sew the longer strips to the sides, adjusting to fit. Add a C piece at the corners as shown in Figure 3. Adjust the angle

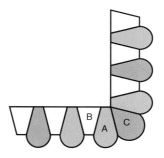

Figure 3
Add C piece at corners as shown.

to make a 90-degree corner if necessary; press.

Step 8. Sew three 3 1/2" x 16 1/2" sashing strips together with four blocks, beginning and ending with a block. Repeat for three rows. Join the rows with the 3 1/2" x 73 1/2" strips referring to the Placement Diagram; press.

Step 9. Cut two green border strips 3 1/2" x 60 1/2" and two strips 3 1/2" x 79 1/2". Sew the short strips to the top and bottom and the long strips to the sides of the completed top, mitering corners; press.

Step 10. Cut two muslin border strips 3 1/2" x 66 1/2" and two strips 3 1/2" x 85 1/2". Sew the short strips to the top and bottom and the long strips to the sides, mitering corners; press.

Step 11. Cut two green border strips 3 1/2" x 72 1/2" and two strips 3 1/2" x 91 1/2". Sew the

Step 15. Choose a quilting design or design one of your own. Mark the design on the top referring to the instructions given on Page 167.

Step 16. Finish quilt referring to Pages 167–175 for instructions.

Tips & Techniques

For many quiltmakers, finishing the edges is a dreaded step. Remember that when this job is complete, your quilt is truly finished.

The edges of the quilt usually receive the most wear and tear. Bias binding is the most durable edge finish because the fabric threads run on the diagonal on the edges and no one thread is exposed to excessive wear. Or, the front edge may be turned to the back and the back edge may be turned to the front. This edge finish is

one of the easiest to execute, but is not as durable.

The edge finish should be neat and add to the beauty of the finished quilt. Too many quilters rush through this process only to find the edges of their quilt ripple and are not square. An untidy edge finish will cancel out hours of careful work on the quilt top. Take your time during this process. You'll be pleased with the fine finishing touch to your quilt.

T-Tulips
Placement Diagram
Approximately 81" x 100"

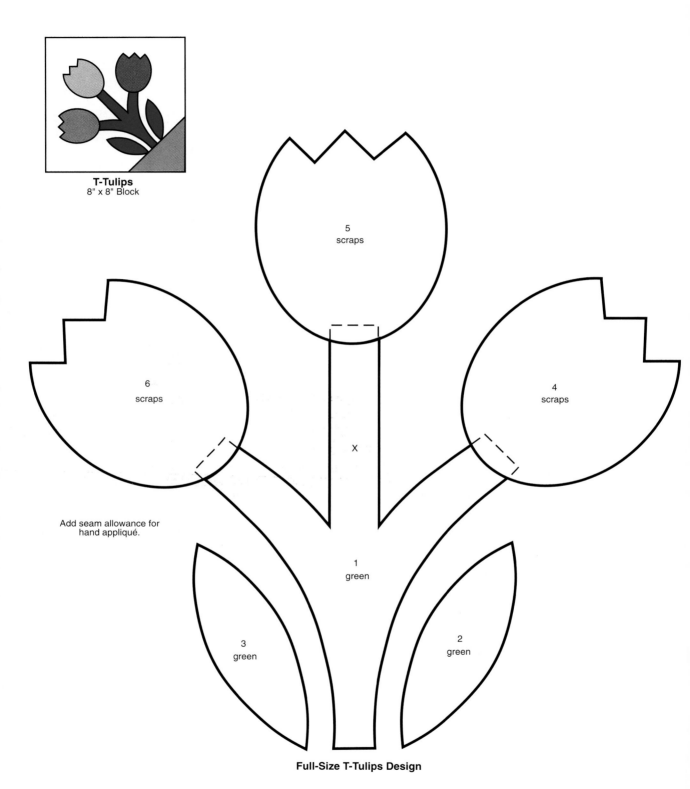

T-Tulips
8" x 8" Block

5
scraps

6
scraps

4
scraps

X

Add seam allowance for
hand appliqué.

1
green

3
green

2
green

Full-Size T-Tulips Design

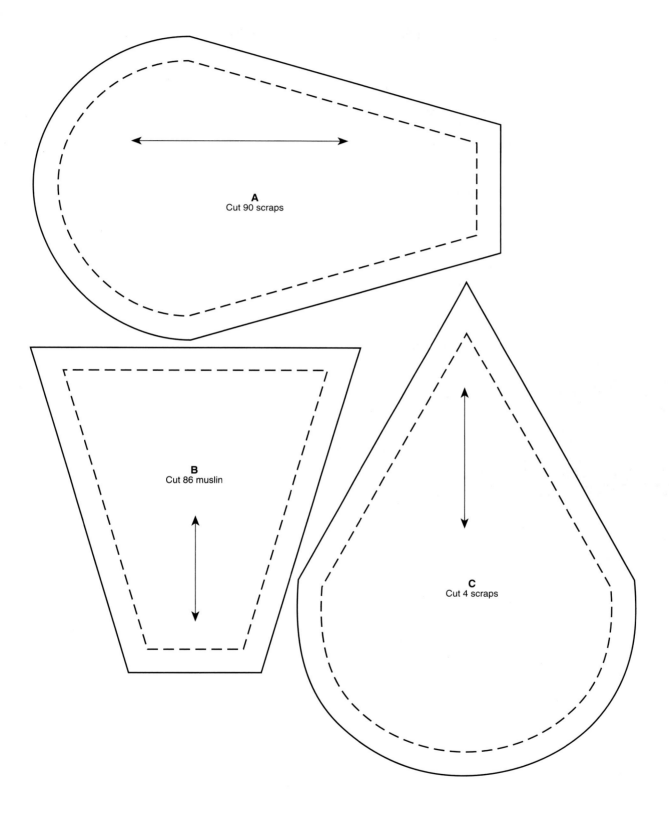

A
Cut 90 scraps

B
Cut 86 muslin

C
Cut 4 scraps

Summer Butterflies

Our grandmothers always had lovely flower gardens, and the gardens always attracted delightful butterflies. So it's only natural that Grandmother would find a way to keep those butterflies around all year long with bright, cheerful butterfly quilts. Add a butterfly quilt to your collection too!

Each butterfly in this beautiful quilt was cut from a different print and carefully appliquéd to background blocks with a buttonhole stitch using black thread. Sunny yellow sashing helps to create a truly summerlike quilt. Gather your favorite floral prints to make one like it. The butterflies will remind you on those chilly winter days that spring and summer are just around the corner.

Instructions

Step 1. Prepare butterfly template using pattern piece given. Cut 54 butterfly shapes from fabric scraps. Add a 1/4" seam allowance to pattern given if you will be turning under the edge for hand appliqué.

Step 2. Cut 54 squares muslin 9" x 9". Fold and crease to mark centers.

Step 3. Center a butterfly shape diagonally on each background block and pin in place.

Step 4. Appliqué the butterfly shapes to background squares using one of the methods discussed on Pages 159–161. The quilt shown uses a buttonhole stitch with 2 or 3 strands of black embroidery floss. Embroider antennae with a stem stitch (see Pages 161 and 162 for stitch instructions).

Step 5. After appliqué is complete, cut four

Quilt Measurements
Quilt Size: 85" x 93 1/2"
Block Size: 8 1/2" x 8 1/2"

Materials
• 4 yards muslin
• 4 yards scraps or 54 pieces 8" square
• 4 yards yellow solid
• 2 skeins black embroidery floss
• Backing 89" x 98"
• Batting 89" x 98"
• 10 yards self-made or purchased red binding

strips yellow 4 3/4" x 26" and four strips 4 3/4" x 51 1/2", two strips 9" x 77" and two strips 9" x 85 1/2".

Step 6. Sew three rows of two blocks each and sew together, referring to the Placement Diagram. Sew a 26" strip to the opposite sides; press; then sew the remaining 26" strips to the top and bottom; press.

Step 7. Make two rows of four butterflies each for each side. Refer to the Placement Diagram for positioning of butterflies. Sew a row to each side of the completed center.

Step 8. Sew two rows with five butterflies

each, referring to the Placement Diagram for placement of butterflies.

Step 9. Sew a 51 1/2" yellow strip to opposite sides; press. Sew the remaining two 51 1/2" strips to the top and bottom; press.

Step 10. Make two side butterfly rows with seven blocks in each strip. Add to sides. Make top and bottom rows with eight blocks and sew to quilt top. Press.

Step 11. Sew 77" yellow strips to opposite sides; press. Sew 85 1/2" strips to top and bottom; press.

Step 12. Choose a quilting design or design one of your own. Mark the design on the top referring to the instructions given on Page 167.

Step 13. Finish quilt referring to Pages 167–175 for instructions.

Summer Butterflies
8 1/2" x 8 1/2" Block

Butterfly
Cut 1 scrap print (54)

Place line on fold

Add seam allowance for hand appliqué.

Embroider on dotted lines with stem stitch and black embroidery floss.

Tips & Techniques

You can be sure that most of our grandmothers did not have a sewing room. It is nice to have a space, but not necessary.

Your sewing area should have both an area to the left and in back of the sewing machine so that excess fabric can lie on the surface around the machine and not drop to the floor during sewing. The weight of the fabric pulls on the needle as you sew and causes it to bend or break. This pressure on the needle can cause damage to the machine. It also causes irregular-sized stitches when sewing.

Set up the iron and ironing board near the sewing area. When sewing lots of little pieces of fabric together, pressing the seam allowances as you sew is more efficient.

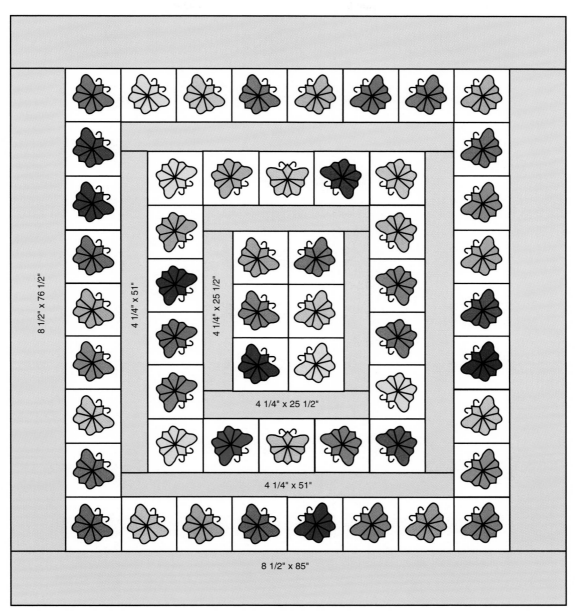

Summer Butterflies
Placement Diagram
85" x 93 1/2"

Sunbonnet Sue & Overall Bill Baby Quilt

This delightful antique crib quilt is a wonderful example of how the Sunbonnet Sue and Overall Bill patterns were combined by our grandmothers to make cuddly baby quilts.

Finding antique crib quilts in good condition is rare because the quilts endured much use and laundering. Be sure to select durable fabrics and batting for your baby quilt so that special little one will still have the quilt to treasure for years to come.

Instructions

Step 1. Prepare templates for each pattern shape using full-size patterns given. For machine appliqué, remember to add a seam allowance to any piece that is placed under another piece such as at the top of the shoe where it is tucked under the dress as indicated by dotted lines. Refer to Pages 159 and 160 for appliqué instructions.

Step 2. Cut fabric patches as directed on each piece for one block. You will need six each *Sunbonnet Sue* and *Overall Bill* blocks to complete the quilt as shown.

Step 3. Cut 12 muslin background blocks 9 1/2" x 9 1/2". Fold and crease to mark centers. Using a light source and full-size patterns, lightly mark placement of pieces on background, matching center on pattern (marked with an X), and center on background block.

Step 4. Turn under edges on each appliqué shape and stitch down with short running stitches using 1 or 2 strands of black embroi-

Quilt Measurements		
Quilt Size: 40" x 51 1/2"		**Block Size:** 9" x 9"

Materials
• 1 1/4 yards bleached muslin
• 2 yards bright pink solid
• Scraps of prints for dresses, pants and hats; scraps of matching solids for shirts, hats, arms and shoes
• 1 skein black embroidery floss
• Batting 44" x 55"
• Backing 44" x 55"
• 8 yards self-made or purchased binding

dery floss. Do not fold under edges where the piece will be layered under another piece. ***Note:*** *If you prefer, other methods of appliqué may be used.*

Step 5. Place appliqué shapes on background blocks, centering designs and layering. The numbers on the drawings show the order of placement.

Step 6. Appliqué pieces to background with small invisible stitches and thread to match fabrics. When all blocks are appliquéd, set aside.

Step 7. Cut nine pink sashing strips 3" x 9 1/2". Join three strips with four appliquéd blocks referring to the Placement Diagram. Make three rows of four blocks each. Press.

Step 8. Cut two pink strips 3" x 44" and stitch between the rows to join. Press.

Step 9. Cut two pink strips 4 1/2" x 40 1/2" and two strips 4 1/2" x 52".

Step 10. Sew shorter strips to the top and bottom and longer strips to sides, mitering corners; press. Using the scallop pattern given, cut border edges in scalloped shape.

Step 11. Using a water-erasable marker or pencil, mark quilting lines using patterns given. Refer to Figures 1 and 2. Background blocks are quilted in diagonal lines about 1" apart.

Figure 1
Place quilting designs on sashing strips as shown.

Figure 2
Quilting on appliquéd blocks.

Step 12. Prepare for quilting and finish referring to Pages 167–175.

Overall Bill
9" x 9" Block

Sunbonnet Sue
9" x 9" Block

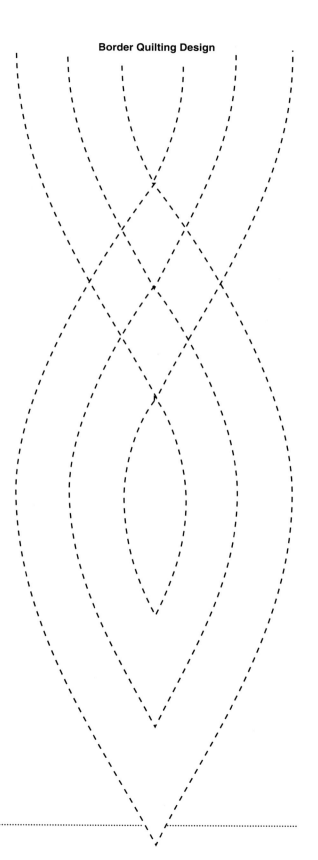

Border Quilting Design

**Sashing Strip
Quilting Design**

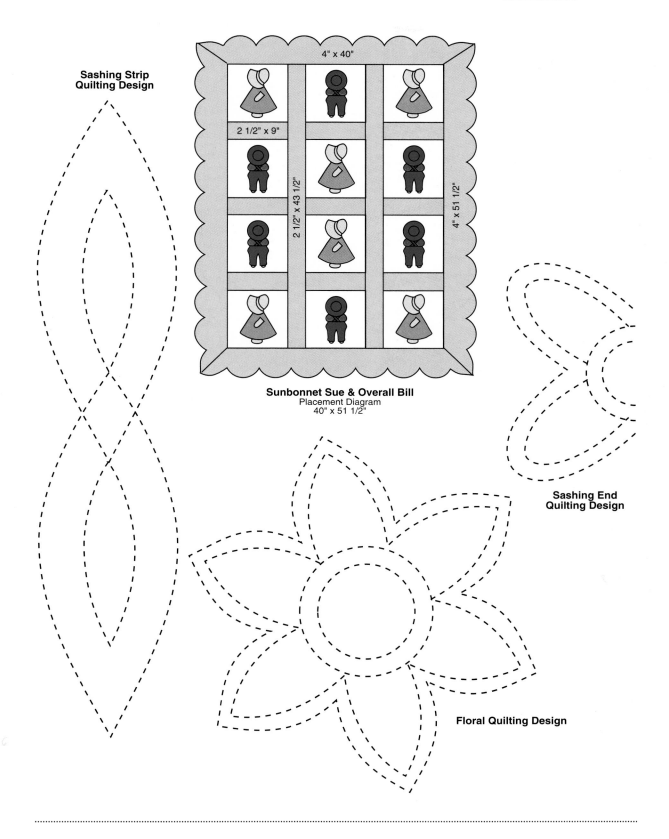

Sunbonnet Sue & Overall Bill
Placement Diagram
40" x 51 1/2"

**Sashing End
Quilting Design**

Floral Quilting Design

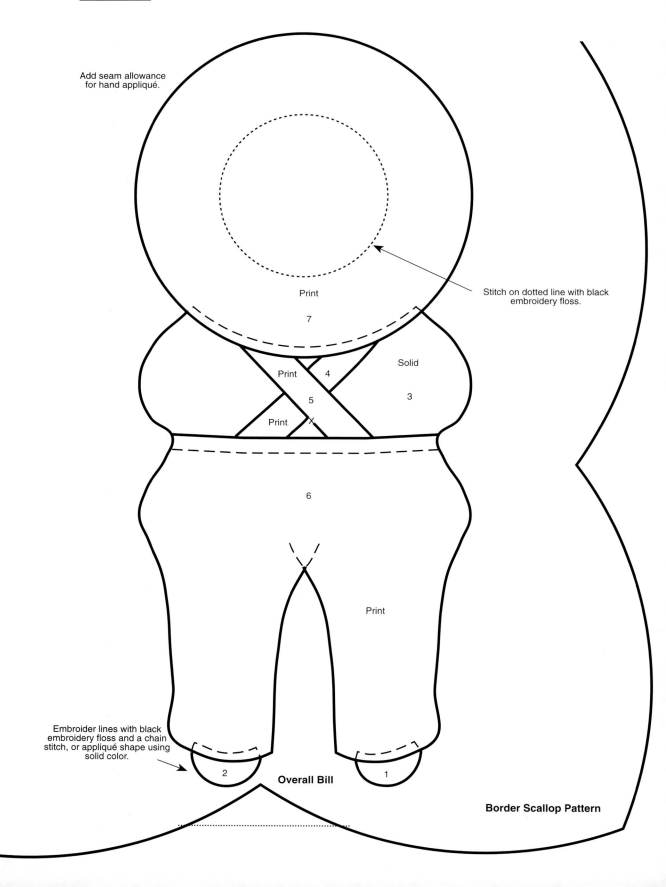

Add seam allowance
for hand appliqué.

Print

7

Stitch on dotted line with black
embroidery floss.

Print

4

Solid

5

3

Print

X

6

Print

Embroider lines with black
embroidery floss and a chain
stitch, or appliqué shape using
solid color.

2

1

Overall Bill

Border Scallop Pattern

Sunbonnet Sue

3

Solid

Stitch on dotted lines with black
embroidery floss.

Add seam allowance
for hand appliqué.

X

Solid

4

2

Print

Solid

1

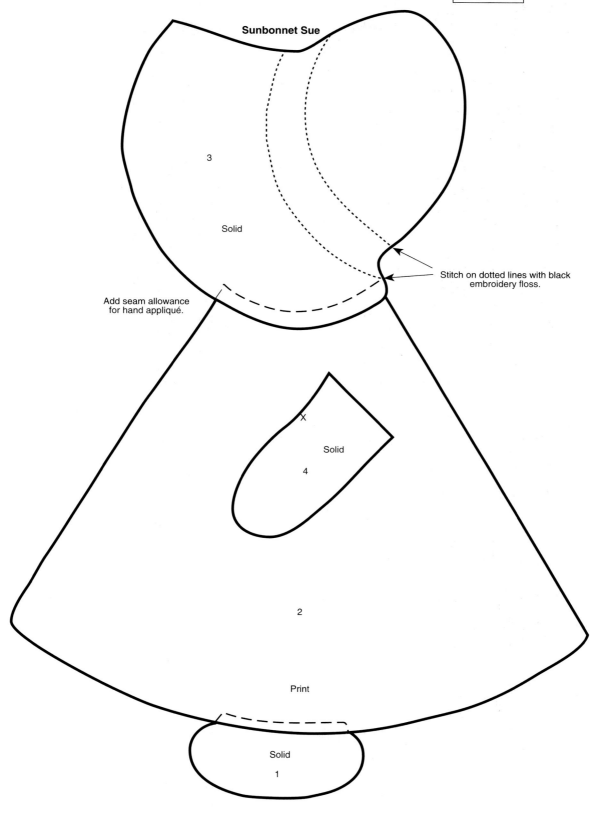

Combination
& Unusual Quilts

Many quilts combine piecing and appliqué and other techniques.

Grandmother often liked to stitch these combinations, which included cross-stitch, embroidery, white-on-white and embellished.

You'll especially enjoy our lovely old quilt made with beautiful handkerchiefs, a perfect way to display those treasured keepsakes from yesterday.

Although the miniature quilt was not made in the 1930s like most of the other quilts in this book, it was made with vintage 1930s fabrics.

If you can find some old fabrics don't hesitate to use them!

Tips & Techniques for
❧Combination❧
& Unusual Quilts

Not all quilts are pieced or appliquéd. Grandmother often tried other methods.

Most of the embroidered or cross-stitched quilts made by our grandmothers were created from kits or used iron-on transfer designs. Kits for such quilts are still sold today by mail order catalog companies. Although they are not as popular today as they were then, there are still stitchers who prefer to embroider. Quilting is secondary to them when making a quilt.

Whether you prefer to piece, appliqué, embroider or use other methods, good basic skills are required. If you enjoy working with your hands to create beautiful heirlooms, you can't go wrong when you choose to make a quilt from these lovely patterns from the 1930s.

Fabrics. If using vintage fabrics or feed sack materials, wash and test the fabric's strength. Interesting quilts can be made using reproduction 1930s fabrics.

Marking Tools and Techniques. Be careful when marking designs on the background. Remember that the marks should not be visible when the quilt is finished.

• Marking around templates for cutting requires a sharp, very fine-point pencil. A No. 2 lead pencil is recommended for this job. Sharpen your pencils often to keep the point sharp. Accuracy when cutting fabric pieces is essential.

• When marking on the right side of the fabric as for some appliqué techniques, be very careful to use a pencil or marker that won't show when sewing is finished.

• If pens are used to mark on the wrong side of the fabric, be careful when sewing with light-colored thread as the thread will pick up color from the ink during the sewing process.

• Grandmother probably used a pencil or the tip of her needle to mark her designs on the quilt top, but today we have many available products in addition to the No. 2 lead pencil. Other popular marking choices include a silver drawing pencil and a white chalk pencil.

• Wash-out markers are popular with some quilters, while others do not recommend them. The advantage to their use is that the color washes out when the quilting is complete. The disadvantage is that the chemicals may remain in the fabric after washing. This could cause damage to the fabric and/or discoloration at a later date.

• Take special care that your finished quilt shows no evidence of any marks.

Be sure to read General Instructions for Quiltmaking, beginning on Page 152, for more tips and techniques to help you make a quilt that will become a keepsake.

Fancy Dresden Plate

These two beautiful twin-size tops were never finished.
It may be a comfort to some of us to discover that our grandmothers sometimes
had as much trouble completing their quilt projects as we do today!
The blocks are very well made, crisp, clean and neatly hand-stitched together.

The *Dresden Plate* quilt tops shown have been embellished with the addition of the four green dividing pieces and the curved green center pieces. The solid green gives these tops away as being made in the 1930s. The tops could be combined, bordered and finished as a king-size quilt or finished as is for matching twin bed quilts.

Instructions

Step 1. Prepare templates and choose method of appliqué referring to Pages 158–160 for instructions.

Step 2. Cut 15 background blocks 16 1/2" x 16 1/2" (larger, if desired; trim to size when appliqué is complete).

Step 3. Fold blocks in half and in half again; crease to mark center lines. Unfold and fold on the diagonals; crease to mark.

Step 4. Draw a 5 1/2" circle in the center of the block lightly with water-erasable marker or pencil. This circle is the guideline for placement of A pieces.

Step 5. Sew four A pieces together; repeat for four A units. Press seams to one side. Join these four units with B. Adjust if necessary to

Quilt Measurements
Quilt Size: 48" x 80"   **Block Size:** 16" x 16"

Materials
For each quilt: • 4 yards white for background   • 1/2 yard green solid   • Variety of print scraps   • Backing 52" x 84"   • Batting 52" x 84"   • 7 1/2 yards self-made or purchased binding

make circle shape lie flat.

Step 6. Pin the pieced shape to the background, matching crease lines to B pieces. Baste in place around outside edges. Place piece C under raw edge of the center of the pieced unit, matching up seam lines. Do not turn in edge of C. Baste in place.

Step 7. Appliqué circular unit and C in place on background block using chosen method. Repeat for 15 blocks for each quilt.

Step 8. Arrange the blocks in five rows of three blocks each; join in rows; join rows to complete the top; press.

Step 9. Borders may be added at this time, if desired.

Step 10. Finish quilt as desired referring to Pages 167–175 for basic instructions.

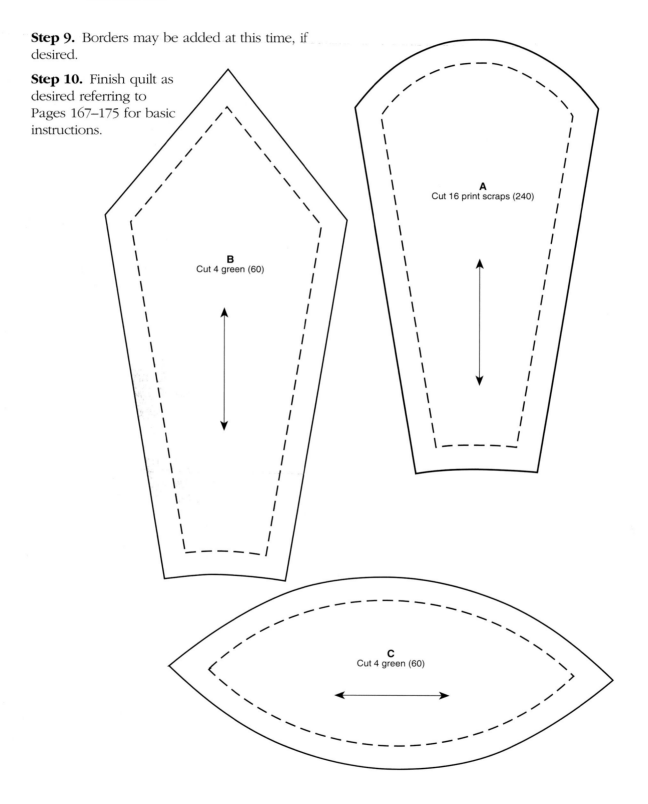

B
Cut 4 green (60)

A
Cut 16 print scraps (240)

C
Cut 4 green (60)

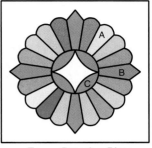

Fancy Dresden Plate
16" x 16" Block

Fancy Dresden Plate
Placement Diagram
48" x 80"

Hearts & Gizzards

Martha Wolford was given this lovely quilt by her aunt, one of many quilts made by her two maiden great-aunts in their lifetime. Her aunt told her the date was on the quilt but she hadn't been able to find it. By accident, as Martha folded the quilt over a chair one day, she noticed the date, 1938, stitched in one corner, white thread on white fabric. What a thrill for Martha to discover that the quilt was made the year she was born!

This interesting quilt pattern uses only two colors to make a beautiful quilt, the perfect complement for a room with busy wallpaper. As a block the corner pieces combine to make heart shapes. When blocks are set together as shown on this quilt top, the corner heart designs make a cheerful floral pattern.

Instructions

Step 1. Prepare templates and cut pieces referring to Pages 154–156.

Step 2. To piece one block, sew a white A to a pink A. Sew a white B to a pink B, referring to Figure 1. Repeat, reversing the colors. Appliqué the B units to opposite corners of the A unit. Trim away excess A from the back after appliqué is complete to reduce bulk, if desired. Complete 56 blocks; press.

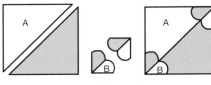

Figure 1
Piece 1 block as shown.

Quilt Measurements
Quilt Size: 77" x 86"   **Block Size:** 9" x 9"

Materials
• 5 yards pink solid
• 10 yards white (includes backing)
• Batting 80" x 90"
• 9 1/2 yards purchased or self-made binding

Step 3. Arrange blocks in eight rows with seven blocks in each row. As the blocks are stitched together you will see that a heart-shaped design emerges in the corners.

Step 4. Cut two pink border strips 3" x 63 1/2" and add to top and bottom. Cut two pink strips 3" x 77 1/2" and add to opposite sides.

Step 5. Cut two white strips 3" x 68 1/2" and add to top and bottom and two strips 3" x 82 1/2" and add to opposite sides.

Step 6. Cut two pink strips 2 1/2" x 73 1/2" and add to top and bottom. Cut two pink strips 2 1/2" x 86 1/2" and add to opposite sides to complete finished quilt top.

Step 7. Choose a quilting design or design one of your own. Mark the design on the top referring to the instructions given on Page 167.

Step 8. Finish quilt referring to Pages 167–175 for instructions.

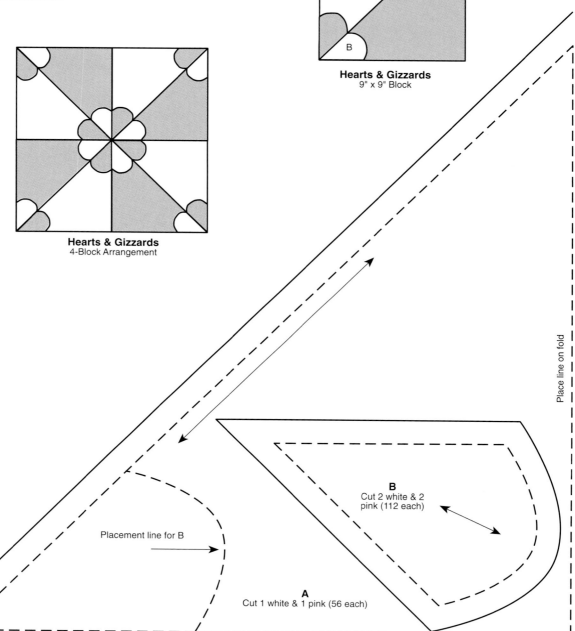

Hearts & Gizzards
9" x 9" Block

Hearts & Gizzards
4-Block Arrangement

Place line on fold

Placement line for B

B
Cut 2 white & 2 pink (112 each)

A
Cut 1 white & 1 pink (56 each)

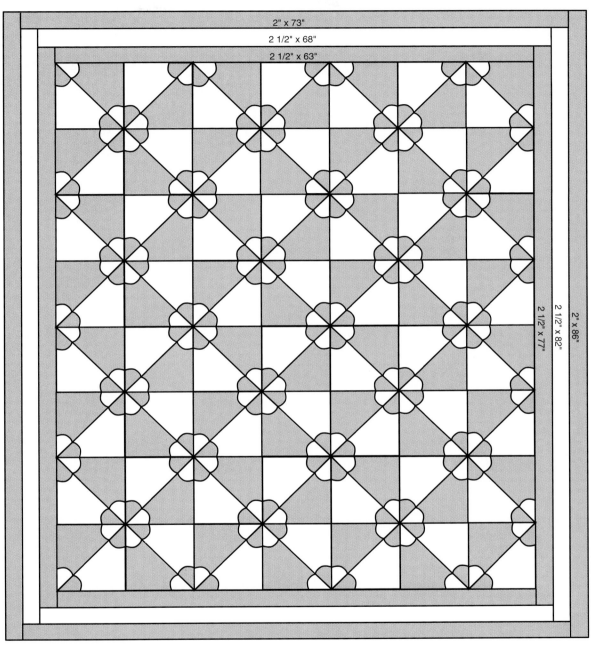

Hearts & Gizzards
Placement Diagram
77" x 86"

Antique Sunflower Quilt

This striking quilt top was purchased at an antique show in Moline, Illinois. Some fabrics date from the mid-1800s, and some of the sashing fabrics date from a later era. The creative quiltmaker pieced strips to join blocks and appliquéd the pieced sunflower designs to solid background blocks, a good combination of techniques.

The top is made up of 16 blocks which were meticulously pieced by hand. The quiltmaker was an expert, sewing 10–15 stitches per inch with a backstitch and 1/8" seams. The quilt top is in excellent condition considering its age. It has only a few minor flaws in some of the darker fabrics.

Consider adding a matching border with additional *Flying Geese* strips to increase the size of the quilt; or try adding coordinating border strips of unpieced fabrics to enlarge the quilt to any size desired.

Instructions

Step 1. To complete one block, sew B to C to A to make a unit referring to Figure 1. Repeat for 22 units. Join these units matching seams at points to form a circle; press.

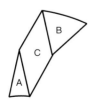

Figure 1
Sew B to C to A as shown. Repeat for 22 units.

Quilt Measurements
Quilt Size: 76" x 76" (without borders)
Block Size: 16" x 16"

Materials
Note: Because this is a scrap quilt, all fabric estimates are approximate.

- Muslin—approximately 10 yards for blocks and sashing
- 6 yards scraps, predominantly brown
- Backing 80" x 80"
- Batting 80" x 80"
- 10 yards self-made or purchased binding

Step 2. Cut 16 muslin squares 16 1/2" x 16 1/2". Fold each square in half in all directions and crease to mark centers.

Step 3. Appliqué the pieced circle to the center of one of the 16 1/2" x 16 1/2" muslin squares, turning under edges as you stitch. Repeat for 16 blocks.

Step 4. Cut D and E triangles as directed on each piece. Sew two E pieces to D to piece one unit as shown in Figure 2. Sew 12 D-E

Sunflower Quilt

Like the quilt that now wraps me,

The ground is fluffy and light,

Spread thick with white crystals

That fell in the night.

Snow covers the garden

Where my sunflowers grew,

Only splinters and stalks show

Where the blossoms stood true.

I sewed all these sunflowers when

I planted their seed,

Choosing colors from memory

and packets of seed.

As the garden developed

I preserved and canned,

But these sunflowers were captured

With fabrics, by hand.

I quilted these flowers

As the stalks blossomed high,

And finished my quilt

When their heads were dry.

Now that winter's upon us,

I've my sunflower bouquet

That's preserved for all seasons

And won't fade away.

— *By Mallory Mares Hoffman*

strips with eight units per strip. Sew three strips with 38 units per strip.

Figure 2
Piece D-E units as shown.

Step 5. Sew four blocks together with the short D-E units. Repeat for four rows. Join the rows with the longer D-E units. Press. ***Note:*** *A larger quilt may be made by adding more E-D units on outside edges for borders.*

Step 6. Choose a quilting design or design one of your own. Mark the design on the top referring to the instructions given on Page 167.

Step 7. Finish quilt referring to Pages 167–175 for instructions.

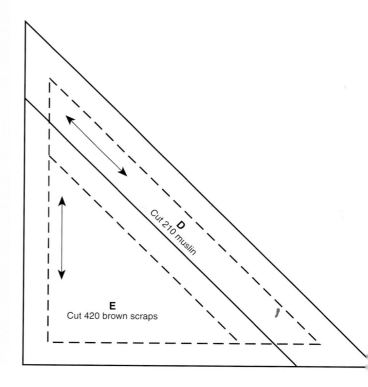

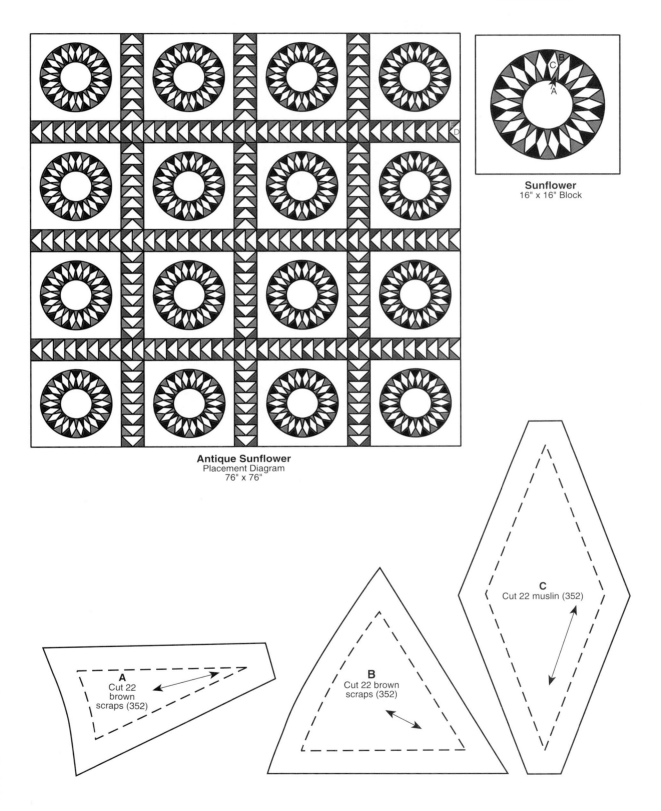

Sunflower
16" x 16" Block

Antique Sunflower
Placement Diagram
76" x 76"

A
Cut 22
brown
scraps (352)

B
Cut 22 brown
scraps (352)

C
Cut 22 muslin (352)

Sweet Sunbonnet Sue

We already shared the pattern for a crib-size Overall Bill & Sunbonnet Sue quilt in Chapter Three, but because Sue was such a popular pattern in the 1930s, we want to share another example of this old favorite in a different form.

Use this pretty *Sunbonnet Sue* pattern to make a twin-size quilt for an older child using fabrics from her outgrown dresses. You need only 20 blocks to make this lovely quilt, which is made larger by the pieced sashing strips joining the blocks together.

Instructions

Step 1. Cut two muslin border strips 7" x 78" and two strips 4 1/2" x 62". Set aside. ***Note:*** *These strips are cut longer than necessary. They are cut now so that they can be one piece instead of being seamed from several pieces.* Cut 20 background blocks from muslin 11" x 11". Fold and crease to mark center of each block.

Step 2. Using full-size pattern given and referring to the instructions on Pages 158 and 159, make templates for each pattern and cut each shape as directed on the piece.

Step 3. Transfer the complete pattern to the background squares, again referring to Pages 158 and 159 for suggestions.

Step 4. Place each appliqué piece in place on background square in numerical order, layering as necessary. Appliqué each piece in place referring to the instructions as before.

Step 5. When appliqué is complete, embroider details. Refer to Pages 161 and 162 for instructions.

Quilt Measurements

Quilt Size: 72 1/2" x 81 1/2"
Block Size: 10 1/2" x 10 1/2"

Materials

- 5 yards muslin
- 2 yards solid light blue
- Scraps coordinating solids and prints for hats and dresses
- Embroidery floss to match scraps
- Backing 76" x 86"
- Batting 76" x 86"
- 9 yards self-made or purchased binding

Step 6. When blocks are complete, set aside.

Step 7. Piece one sashing unit referring to Figure 1. Repeat for 49 units; press.

Figure 1
Piece 1 sashing unit as shown.

Step 8. Arrange four blocks with five sashing

units as shown in Figure 2 to complete one row. Repeat for five rows. Sew in rows; press seams toward sashing strips.

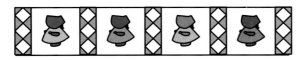

Figure 2
Join sashing units with blocks to make rows as shown.

Step 9. Sew five E squares together with four sashing units referring to Figure 3. Repeat for six sashing-unit rows. Press seams toward sashing units.

Figure 3
Join sashing units with E to make rows as shown.

Step 10. Join the block rows with the sashing-unit rows referring to the Placement Diagram to complete inner pieced section.

Step 11. Cut two muslin border strips 7" x 74".

Note: *This border size is the exact size needed if all sewing is accurate. Measure your own quilt top before trimming the previously cut border strips to the proper size before sewing.* Sew one to each long side of top center. Press seams toward border strips.

Step 12. Cut two muslin border strips 4 1/2" x 60". Sew a D piece to each end. Press seams toward D. Sew a strip to the top and bottom. Press seams toward border strips to finish.

Step 13. Choose a quilting design for the border or mark straight

lines 1" apart as shown on the quilt. Refer to Page 167 for marking instructions. The blocks were quilted on the diagonal in both directions and around the appliqué shapes. The sashing units were quilted 1/4" away from seams in each piece.

Step 14. Layer the backing and batting with the completed top and prepare for quilting referring to Pages 167 and 168.

Step 15. Finish quilt as desired referring to Pages 169–175.

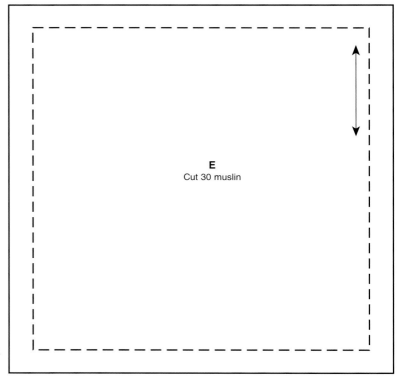

Sweet Sunbonnet Sue
Placement Diagram
72 1/2" x 81 1/2"

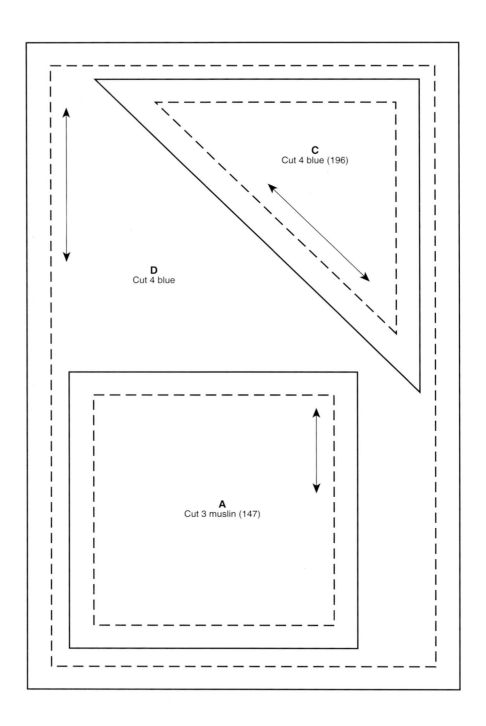

C
Cut 4 blue (196)

D
Cut 4 blue

A
Cut 3 muslin (147)

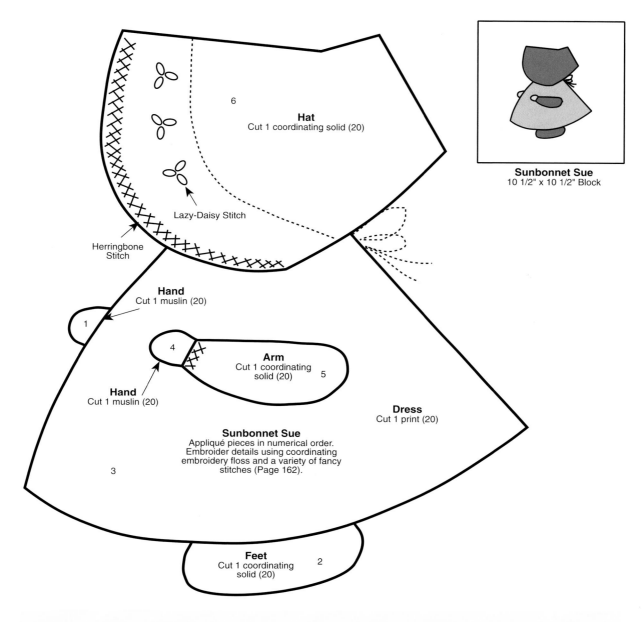

6

Hat
Cut 1 coordinating solid (20)

Lazy-Daisy Stitch

Herringbone
Stitch

Hand
Cut 1 muslin (20)

1

4

Arm
Cut 1 coordinating
solid (20)

5

Hand
Cut 1 muslin (20)

Dress
Cut 1 print (20)

Sunbonnet Sue
Appliqué pieces in numerical order.
Embroider details using coordinating
embroidery floss and a variety of fancy
stitches (Page 162).

3

Feet
Cut 1 coordinating
solid (20)

2

Sunbonnet Sue
10 1/2" x 10 1/2" Block

Tips & Techniques

Quilts with blocks set on the diagonal often use plain blocks between pieced blocks and plain corner and fill-in triangles. These all may be cut using a rotary cutter and faster methods as described. Notice that the quarter-square fill-in triangles have the straight of grain on the outside edges and the corner triangles have the straight of grain on both sides. The general rule is to keep the outside edges of blocks on quilts on the straight of grain. This will reduce stretching during the finishing processes and keep the quilt square.

Morning Glory

Sometimes the quilt patterns from our grandmothers' era do not even remotely resemble the names given to them. In this case, however, the flower is unmistakably a morning glory, a lovely flower that grew in every flower garden back then. This colorful quilt is a fine example of how scraps can be used to make a flower garden of fabrics.

The *Morning Glory* pattern is unusual because the floral design was pieced and not appliquéd, as it appears. The leaves were appliquéd with dark green embroidered veins, but the flower shape was pieced. The variety of fabric scraps used to make the flower blocks add a sparkle of color to this interesting pieced quilt design.

Instructions

Step 1. To complete one block, sew B to C to D. Repeat three times. Set these four units together with piece A referring to Figure 1.

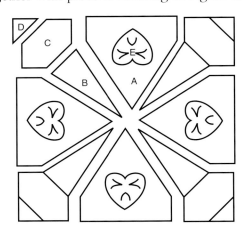

Figure 1
Piece block as shown.

Step 2. Appliqué piece E in center of A pieces and embroider on the marked lines with green

Quilt Measurements
Quilt Size: 77" x 91 3/4"
Block Size: 11 1/2" x 11 1/2"

Materials

- 8 yards white
- 1 yard green
- Assorted scraps for flower pattern
- 2 skeins green and 1 skein yellow embroidery floss
- Backing 80" x 98"
- Batting 80" x 98"
- 10 yards self-made or purchased binding

floss using a stem stitch. Embroider the design shown on the C piece with yellow floss in the stem stitch.

Step 3. Complete 30 blocks; press.

Step 4. Cut 42 sashing squares 3 3/4" x 3 3/4" from green. Cut 71 sashing strips 3 3/4" x 12" from white.

Step 5. Sew a strip consisting of five blocks and six sashing strips, beginning and ending with a strip. Repeat for six strips. Set aside.

Step 6. Sew six sashing squares to five sashing strips, beginning and ending with a square.

Complete seven of these strips.

Step 7. Referring to the Placement Diagram, lay out the strips and the sashed blocks in rows and sew together; begin and end with sashing-strip rows.

Step 8. When your top is complete, press and prepare for marking. The quilt shown is quilted in a diamond-shape design in the sashing strip and outline-quilted on the blocks.

Step 9. Mark the design on the top referring to the instructions given on Page 167.

Step 10. Finish quilt referring to Pages 167–175 for instructions.

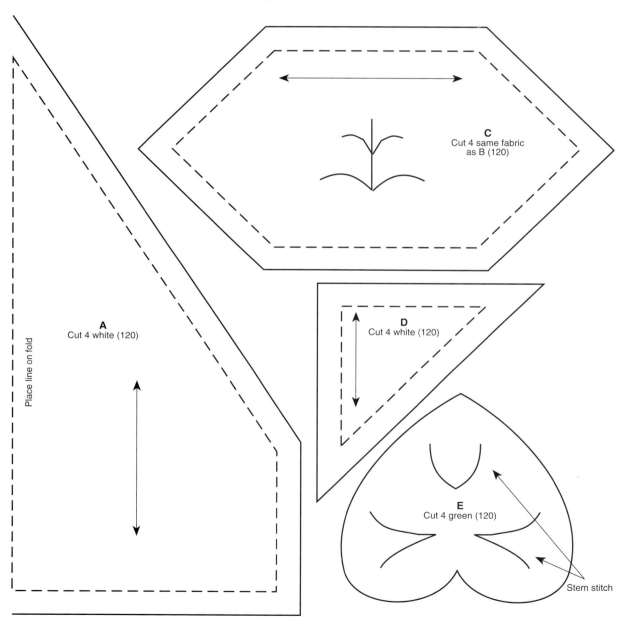

C
Cut 4 same fabric
as B (120)

A
Cut 4 white (120)

Place line on fold

D
Cut 4 white (120)

E
Cut 4 green (120)

Stem stitch

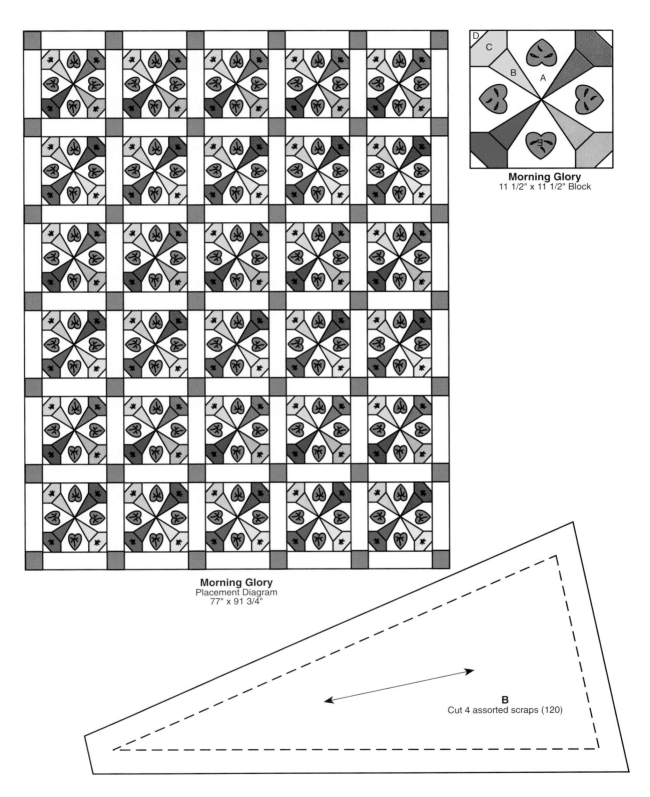

Morning Glory
11 1/2" x 11 1/2" Block

Morning Glory
Placement Diagram
77" x 91 3/4"

B
Cut 4 assorted scraps (120)

Dresden Plate

One of the most popular patterns ever made into quilts has been the Dresden Plate. Most of our grandmothers found themselves with small amounts of a wide variety of fabrics, and a versatile design such as this was just right for what they had on hand. The pattern is a great beginner block because you learn so much from making one.

Because it combines both piecing and appliqué techniques, much can be learned from piecing just one *Dresden Plate* block. It requires precision piecing for all of the pieces to lie down flat once they are stitched together. Lessons are learned about seam allowances, basting, centering the design on the block, appliqué stitching and color combination.

The *Dresden Plate* design is found in many forms. It can be seen with round edges on the sections or with pointed ones. It can have as few as eight sections or as many as 32. The more you have, the harder it is to get it to come out right! It can be in planned colors or it can use scraps. There is so much you can do when working with this design.

Several versions of this versatile design have been included in this book. When you have mastered a perfect *Dresden Plate* block, most other patterns will not present such a challenge to you.

Instructions
Step 1. Cut the number of pieces suggested on your chosen template shape for each block.

Step 2. Cut a background block at least 14 1/2" square; fold to find the center. Finger-press to make lines for positioning quarter sections of

Quilt Measurements
Quilt Size: 84" x 98"
Block Size: 14" x 14"

Materials
• 7 yards background fabric
• Scraps of contrasting prints
• Backing 88" x 102"
• Batting 88" x 102"
• 10 1/2 yards self-made or purchased binding

the finished design.

Step 3. Start piecing the sections either in one continuous circle or in quarters; join the quarters to complete the design.

Note: *If the shape will not lie flat, take in a few of the seams where needed.*

Step 4. Baste outer and inner edges under 1/4". Center on block, using creased lines as guides for placement. Baste in place.

Note: *A fabric circle may be appliquéd to the center. If using a fabric circle, do not turn inside edges of plate shapes under when applying to the background block.*

Step 5. Appliqué pieced plates down with a blind stitch or appliqué stitch.

Step 6. Complete as many blocks as necessary to construct a quilt of the desired size; or make into a pillow using one or two blocks.

Step 7. Blocks may be sashed or set block to block. Refer to Pages 163 and 164 for setting choices.

Step 8. Finish quilt referring to Pages 165–175.

Dresden Plate
14" x 14"
This Dresden Plate has 20 sections which are pointed on the tops.

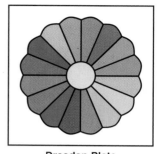

Dresden Plate
14" x 14"
This Dresden Plate has 16 sections which are round on the tops.

Tips & Techniques

Pins are used to hold fabric layers together before sewing. There are several types available, but for quilting, long, thin straight pins are best. They don't leave a large hole and are easier to put in and out of the fabric. Good pins are hard to find and very expensive. A box of fine-quality pins can cost more than $6!

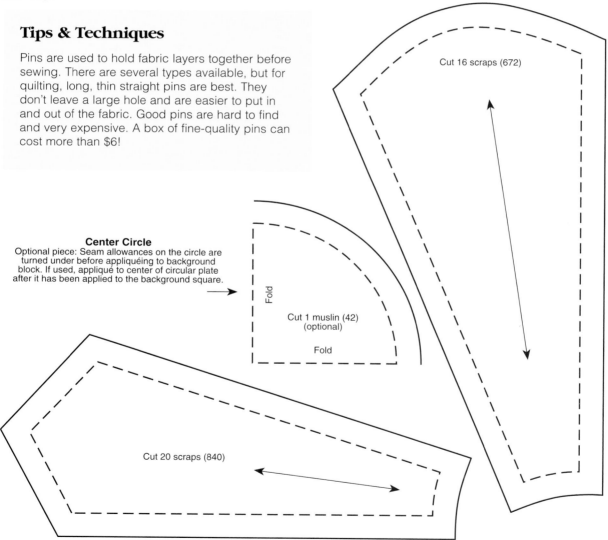

Cut 16 scraps (672)

Center Circle
Optional piece: Seam allowances on the circle are turned under before appliquéing to background block. If used, appliqué to center of circular plate after it has been applied to the background square.

Fold

Cut 1 muslin (42)
(optional)

Fold

Cut 20 scraps (840)

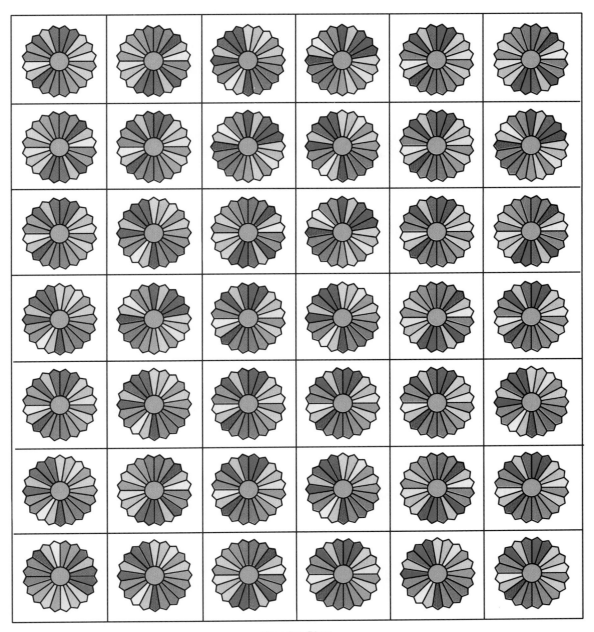

Dresden Plate
Placement Diagram
84" x 98"

Colonial Lady

This lovely pattern is just one of many designs featuring the shape of a woman dressed in her best clothing as if she were out for an evening stroll. The design is perfect for using scraps left over from dressmaking, which is why it was so popular in the 1930s. You can make a modern version using fabrics from today's fashions. Fine-tune your embroidery skills while adding a variety of flowers to each block.

Try to make your ladies colorful and different from one another. You may prefer to cut and appliqué the blocks one at a time. Add flowers as you wish along the bottom of the block. You can also add little pieces of lace and other embellishments to dress up the ladies a bit. Use your imagination! You will need 30 blocks to complete the quilt. **Note:** *The quilt shown varies slightly from the pattern.*

Instructions

Step 1. Cut 30 background blocks from unbleached muslin 14 1/2" x 14 1/2" square.

Step 2. Cut appliqué pieces referring to Page 158 for instructions.

Step 3. Appliqué shapes in place using one of the methods described on Pages 159–161.

Step 4. Complete 30 appliquéd blocks.

Step 5. Embellish flowers with embroidery stitches as desired.

Step 6. Arrange the blocks in a pleasing way, placing colors as you like them.

Step 7. Join the blocks in six rows of five blocks each. Join the rows to complete inner portion of the top; press.

Quilt Measurements

Quilt Size: 79" x 93"
Block Size: 14" x 14"

Materials

- Print and solid scraps for clothing
- 1/8 yard peach solid
- 5 yards unbleached muslin
- 3 yards 90"-wide unbleached muslin for backing and pieced border
- Scraps for pieced border
- Batting 83" x 97"

Step 8. Cut the A, B and C border pieces as directed on pattern pieces.

Step 9. Sew together in rows of approximately 24 triangles on each side and 20 across the top and bottom. Turn the corner with piece C, adjusting size to fit referring to Figure 1. Add border strips to top, working with pieces to make it fit.

Step 10. Choose a quilting design or design one of your own.

Step 11. Mark the design on the top referring to the instructions given on Page 167.

Tips & Techniques

Most of the embroidered or cross-stitched quilts made by our grandmothers were created from kits or iron-on transfer designs. Kits for such quilts are still sold today by mail-order catalog companies. Although they are not as popular today as they were then, there are still stitchers who prefer to embroider.

Step 12. When quilting is complete, trim away *batting only* to edges of quilt. Trim backing 1/2" larger all around.

Step 13. Turn backing to front edge around cone shapes and hand-stitch to backside to finish.

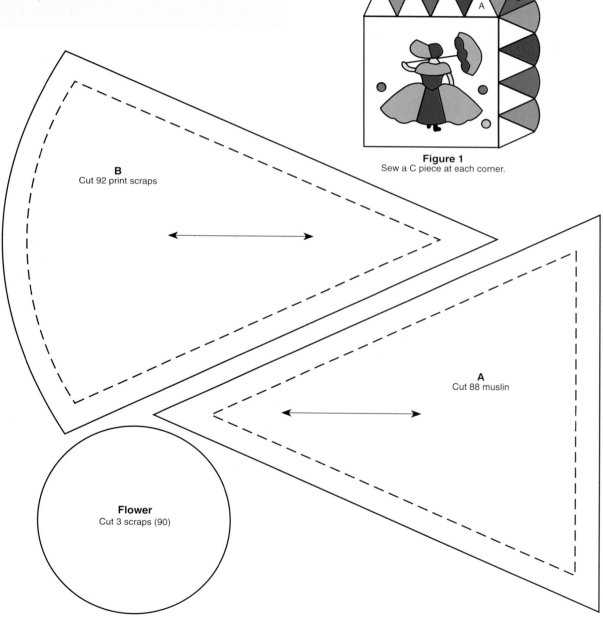

Figure 1
Sew a C piece at each corner.

B
Cut 92 print scraps

A
Cut 88 muslin

Flower
Cut 3 scraps (90)

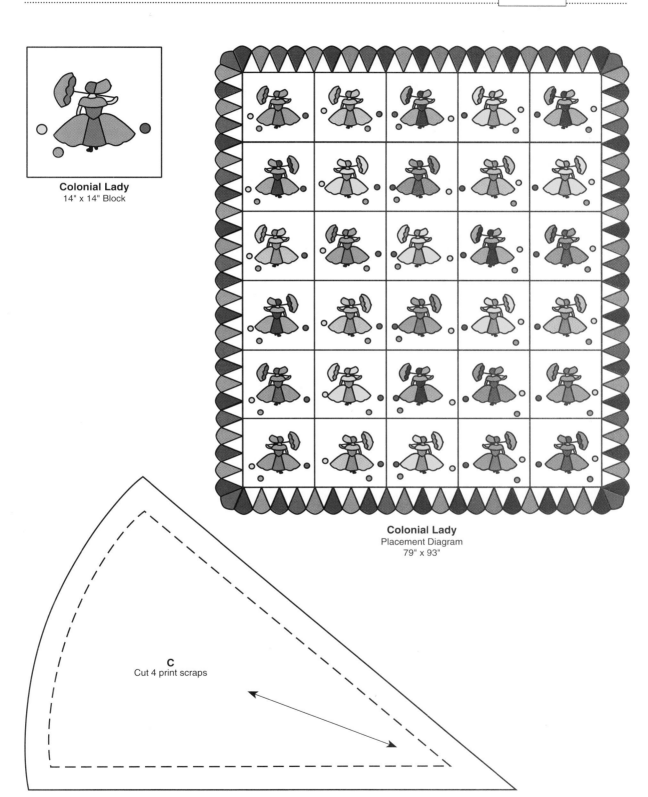

Colonial Lady
14" x 14" Block

Colonial Lady
Placement Diagram
79" x 93"

C
Cut 4 print scraps

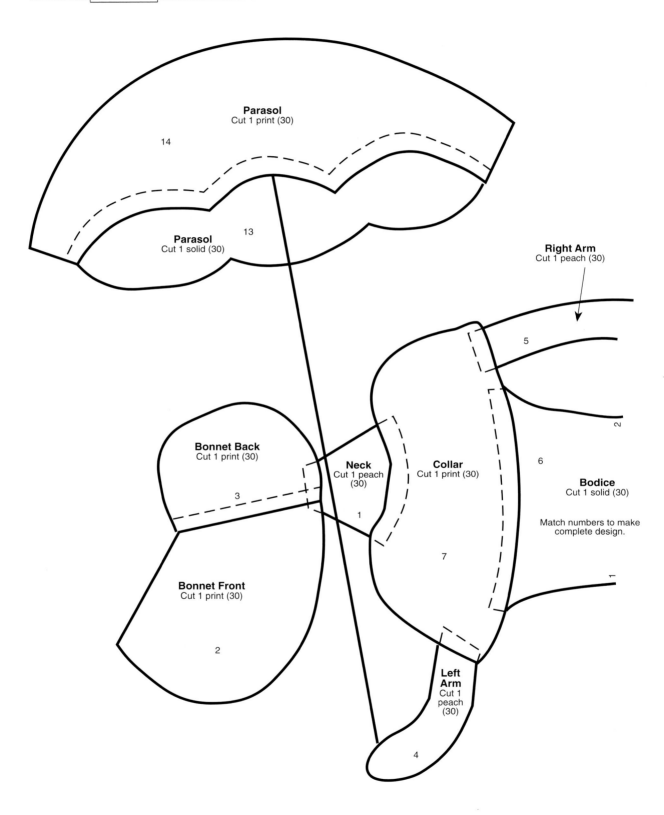

Parasol
Cut 1 print (30)

14

Parasol
Cut 1 solid (30)

13

Right Arm
Cut 1 peach (30)

5

2

Bonnet Back
Cut 1 print (30)

3

Neck
Cut 1 peach
(30)

1

Collar
Cut 1 print (30)

6

Bodice
Cut 1 solid (30)

Match numbers to make
complete design.

7

1

Bonnet Front
Cut 1 print (30)

2

**Left
Arm**
Cut 1
peach
(30)

4

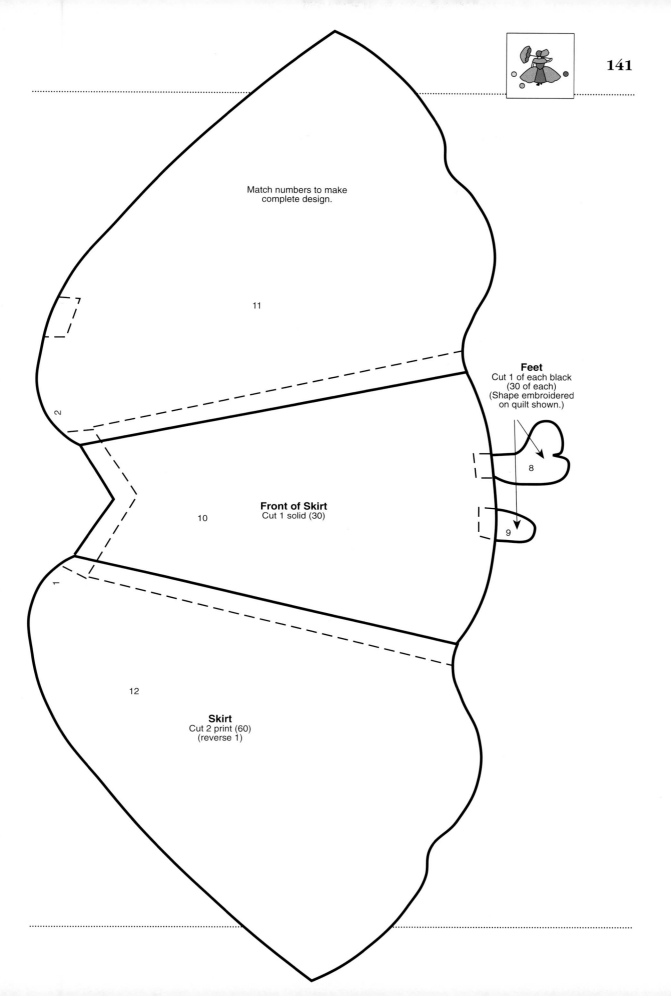

Match numbers to make
complete design.

11

2

Feet
Cut 1 of each black
(30 of each)
(Shape embroidered
on quilt shown.)

8

10

Front of Skirt
Cut 1 solid (30)

9

1

12

Skirt
Cut 2 print (60)
(reverse 1)

Patience Corner

Miniatures are popular in the '90s because they give quilters a chance to use their favorite colors and designs in quilts without a huge investment in time. Not many real miniature quilts exist from Grandmother's era. Although this miniature was made more recently, it used vintage 1930s fabrics.

If you have a collection of old-time fabrics accumulated from family and exchanges with other quilters, you can make a quilt with a nostalgic flavor of whatever size you wish. Combine the vintage fabrics with today's quick-cutting and piecing methods to create a treasured quilted keepsake.

Instructions

Note: Press all seams in the direction of the arrows given on figure drawings. For traditional template-piecing methods, use the full-size drawing of the Patience Corner *block to prepare templates. Piece blocks referring to figure drawings.*

Step 1. Cut each 1 1/2" x 7" strip into four square segments 1 1/2" wide for piece A.

Step 2. Cut the black-and-white strip into four strips 1" x 11" for B and four strips 1" x 14" for C. Stack the 1" x 11" strips and cut six 1 1/2" segments for a total of 24 B segments.

Step 3. Sew A to B; repeat for four units referring to Figure 1.

Step 4. Stack the four black-and-white print 1" x 14" strips and cut six 2" segments from each

Quilt Measurements
Quilt Size: 12" x 16 1/4"
Block Size: 3" x 3"

Materials
Note: Vintage prints were used in the sample shown.
• 1 1/2" x 7" piece each of 6 assorted prints
• 10" x 16" piece of black-and-white print
• 13" x 14" piece of solid maroon
• 11" x 15" piece of medium blue print
• 6" x 18" piece of light peach print for binding
• Backing 14 1/2" x 18 3/4"
• Batting 14 1/2" x 18 3/4"

strip for a total of 24 C segments.

Step 5. Sew a C piece to each A-B unit referring to Figure 2. Repeat for four units.

Step 6. Sew two C-A-B units together twice. Join referring to Figure 3 to make one *Patience Corner* block. Complete six blocks; press and square up to 3 1/2" x 3 1/2" if necessary.

Figure 1
Sew A to B as shown.

Figure 2
Sew C to A-B as shown.

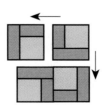

Figure 3
Join the pieced units to
complete 1 block.

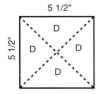

Step 7. From the 13" x 14" piece of solid maroon, cut two 5 1/2" x 5 1/2" squares; cut each square on the diagonal twice to make side fill-in D triangles. Set aside two triangles. Cut two 3 1/2" x 3 1/2" squares for E. Cut two 3" x 3" squares; cut these squares in half on the diagonal once to make F corner triangles. Refer to Figure 4.

Figure 4
Cut 5 1/2" and 3" squares as shown to make
side fill-in D and corner F triangles.

Step 8. Arrange the pieced and solid squares with the D and F triangles in diagonal rows referring to Figure 5.

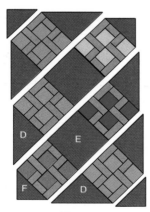

Figure 5
Arrange the pieced blocks with D, E
and F in diagonal rows as shown.

Step 9. Sew the units together in rows; join the rows to complete pieced top. Press seams toward the solid squares and the side D triangles.

Step 10. Cut two border strips from blue print 2 1/4" x 13 1/4"; sew to the long sides of the pieced top. Press seams toward border strips.

Step 11. Cut two more strips blue print 2 1/4" x 12 1/2"; sew to top and bottom of pieced top. Press seams toward border strips.

Step 12. Mark the pieced top for quilting using designs given as suggested or choose a design of your own.

Step 13. Finish the miniature quilt the same as larger quilts. Use a very narrow binding cut only 1" wide. Refer to Pages 167–175 for finishing.

Tips & Techniques

Miniature quilts require scaled-down quilting designs, stitches and binding width. The batting should be very thin. It is possible to separate the layers of some battings to make very thin layers. This is done by carefully pulling the layers apart while trying to keep each layer a consistent thickness. Quilting through such a thin layer of batting makes the execution of tiny quilting stitches a pleasure.

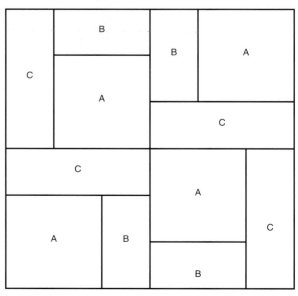

Patience Corner
3" x 3" Block
(Actual Size)

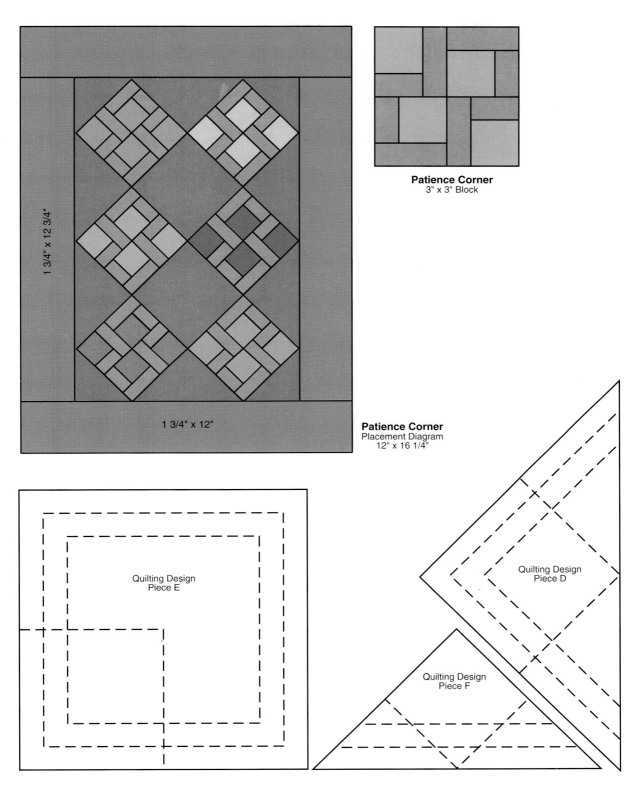

Patience Corner
3" x 3" Block

1 3/4" x 12 3/4"

1 3/4" x 12"

Patience Corner
Placement Diagram
12" x 16 1/4"

Quilting Design
Piece E

Quilting Design
Piece D

Quilting Design
Piece F

Mother's Handkerchiefs

Handkerchiefs are beautiful reminders of people and events.
Our grandmothers knew that their elegant handkerchiefs resembled bright,
graceful butterflies when they were folded crosswise. One quilter found a way to
display her collection by making this fabulous quilt.

If you don't have enough pretty handkerchiefs on hand to make a full-size quilt, you may want to make a smaller project, such as an elegant pillow or a decorative wall quilt. You can often find vintage handkerchiefs at yard sales and flea markets.

Instructions

Step 1. Cut 20 background blocks 13 1/2" x 13 1/2". Fold each block crosswise twice and crease to mark center lines. These lines will be the guides to sew the hankies onto the block.

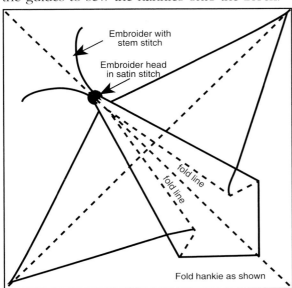

Embroider with stem stitch

Embroider head in satin stitch

fold line
fold line

Fold hankie as shown

Figure 1
Fold hankies and place on background block as shown.

Quilt Measurements	
Quilt Size: 68" x 81"	**Block Size:** 13" x 13"

Materials

- 20 handkerchiefs (try to find some all the same size)
- 6 yards white for background blocks and prairie-point edge
- Various colors of embroidery floss to match handkerchiefs
- Backing 72" x 85"
- Batting 72" x 85"

The point on the bottom of the wings should be on the cross-fold lines and the butterfly's head is located a little beyond the center on the opposite fold line referring to Figure 1.

Step 2. Fold the hankie crosswise, keeping the top hem slightly over the bottom hem. Pin or baste the edges together.

Step 3. Bring a folding pleat toward the center on both sides, overlapping about 1" on the bottom and 1/2" at the top. Both sides should have the same size tucks. This makes the wings of the butterfly angle away from the head. The tip of the wing should touch on the fold line out nearest the edge of the block. The hankie should not go out to the seam line of the block. The pleat forms the butterfly's body and tail.

Step 4. When you have a pleasing shape, pin in place and press lightly with an iron. Do not stretch the hankie in this process.

Step 5. When the hankies have been folded, positioned and basted in place, appliqué down with embroidery floss matching the outer stitched edge of the hankie.

Step 6. Stitch up the pleated section to hold in place using a buttonhole or other stitch that shows on the top of the work. Stitches should be evenly spaced and neat.

Step 7. After the shape has been securely appliquéd in place, embroider a pointed head shape and antennae to each butterfly to

complete. Repeat for 20 blocks.

Step 8. Sew the blocks in four rows of five blocks each. Join the rows to complete the center section of the quilt. Press.

Step 9. Cut two border strips from white 8 1/2" x 68 1/2" and add to the top and bottom. Cut two more strips 8 1/2" x 81 1/2" and add to each side, mitering corners. Press.

Step 10. Mark quilt top with the quilting patterns given.

Step 11. Prepare layers for quilting referring to Pages 167 and 168. Quilt as desired referring to Pages 167–169. Stop quilting stitches at least 1/2" from edge if prairie points will be added to outside edges.

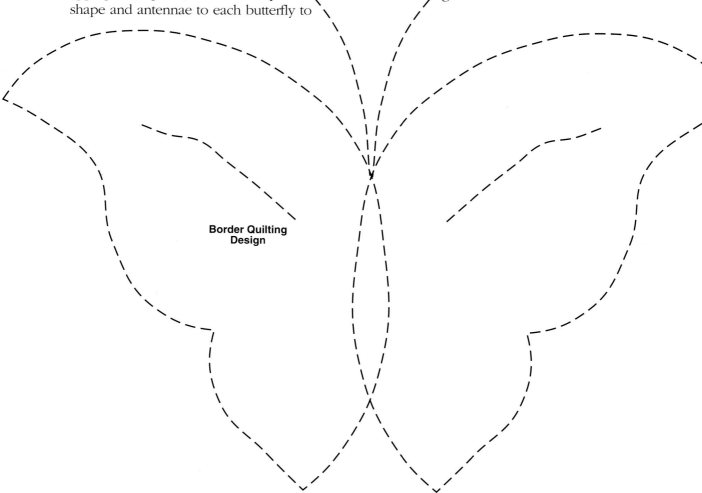

Border Quilting Design

Step 12. Trim batting and backing even with top.

Step 13. To add prairie points, cut 4" squares from white fabric. You will need at least 170 squares to finish around the edge of the quilt.

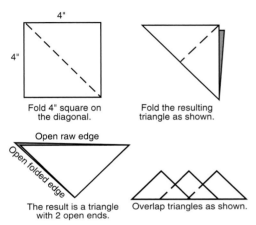

4"

4"

Fold 4" square on the diagonal.

Fold the resulting triangle as shown.

Open raw edge

Open folded edge

The result is a triangle with 2 open ends.

Overlap triangles as shown.

Figure 2
Make prairie-point border sections as shown.

Step 14. Fold the square twice diagonally to result in a triangle with one raw edge as shown in Figure 2. Sew the triangles together in a line, overlapping approximately one-third of the previous triangle. When you have a line long enough to fit on one side, pin it to the quilt top with the top side of the triangle against the sides of the quilt.

Step 15. Sew to the quilt using a 1/4" seam allowance. Do not catch the backing in the seam. When the prairie points have been added all around, turn under backing and blind-stitch to the backside of the quilt, tucking the seam inside to finish.

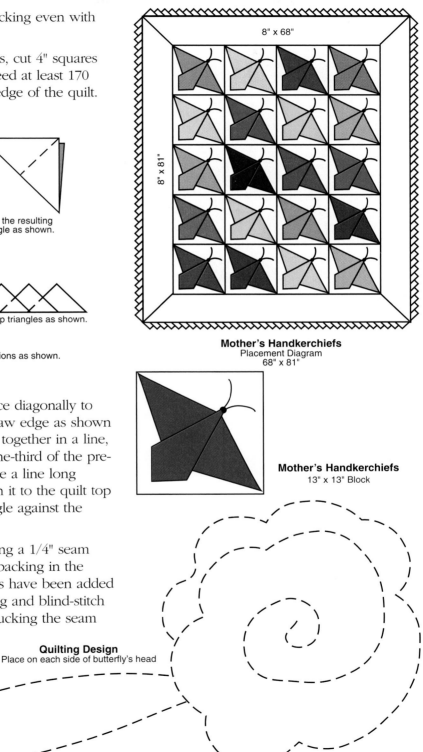

8" x 68"

8" x 81"

Mother's Handkerchiefs
Placement Diagram
68" x 81"

Mother's Handkerchiefs
13" x 13" Block

Quilting Design
Place on each side of butterfly's head

General Instructions

Whether you are a beginner or a seasoned quilter, a quilt from this book will call out for you to pick up your fabric and shears and get busy.

The patterns given here can be adapted to any method. It won't matter if you create every project by hand, or if your sewing machine is your best friend.

Even though our grandmothers didn't have fancy sewing machines or rotary cutters, they were able to make quilts that have withstood the test of time.

Have fun experiencing their creativity as you make these quilt patterns your own!

Materials & Supplies

Editor's Note: No matter which quilt you choose to make from this book, there are some basics you will need to know before you begin. The instructions for specific quilts refer you back to these pages. You will need to have some basic tools, a few skills and the time and inclination to carry your quilt to completion. Using the methods and hints in this section, you will be well on your way to making a quilt that will make your grandmother proud.

Fabrics

The quilts made in the 1930s are recognized for their bright colors—the bright prints, that unusual green solid color, lavenders and orange. These colors are not the most popular today. Although you may find vintage fabrics, there are many reproduction prints available. It is often difficult to tell the difference between the real thing and the reproduction.

Grandmother used fabrics from many sources to make her quilts. You only have to look at the quilts shown in this book to find evidence of their beauty. Feed sacks, grain bags, leftover fabrics and scraps from worn clothing were all recycled for use in quilts. Today feed sacks have become collectible. They are hard to find and expensive to collect.

One hundred percent cotton fabrics are recommended for making quilts. They are durable, crease easily, absorb moisture and generally wear well. Blends are not easily pressed; they do not fade as easily as cotton, but are harder to use in patchwork and appliqué.

Buying Fabrics. Some fabrics have a directional print. Using such fabrics sometimes requires the purchase of more fabric than recommended because special cutting is necessary.

The scale of a print fabric is important. If a print is too large and it has to be cut into very tiny pieces, the design will be lost. When purchasing fabrics, examine the print and consider how it will look when cut into small patches. Will the color be lost? Will the motifs disappear when cut?

Although each pattern has a list of materials needed to construct the quilt as shown, you may already have fabric on hand.

Color. The quilts from the 1930s are, for the most part, bright and cheerful, while quilts from earlier periods were darker. Many of the quilts shown in this book use prints with a white background combined with pastel solids or white because our grandmothers had more of this type of fabric available.

Choose the colors for your quilt using your own color preferences. Trends in fabrics come and go, but your quilt will last for a long time, so you must really love the colors. Remember to choose fabrics that have contrast so that the design will show on the completed quilt.

Preparing the Fabric for Use. Some quilters wash, dry and iron fabrics as soon as they get them home. Others choose not to wash the fabrics at all. Good-quality fabrics are preshrunk and won't shrink much when washed. However, some fabrics will shrink, so you may wish to prewash them to avoid problems after your quilt is completed.

Also, you may want to wash your fabric to determine if it is colorfast. However, prewashing fabric will not guarantee that the dye in the fabric will not run the next time it is washed. Using the home remedies of vinegar or salt-water rinses will only prevent the fabric from running in that wash, not the subsequent washes. Harsh detergents will draw more dye, so try to use a mild soap made especially for quilts and old fabrics. Ask about these products at your local quilt shop.

Quilters who piece by machine don't like to prewash their fabrics. The stiffness in the fabric is considered a plus for machine piecing, and the little bit of shrinking that occurs after the finished quilt is washed helps to hide the actual machine-quilting stitches.

If you decide not to prewash your fabric, test the colorfastness of the darkest fabric in your quilt against the lightest fabric in your quilt. Wash a small piece of both fabrics using the soap you intend to wash the quilt with; let one fabric piece dry on top of the other. If the darkest fabric doesn't run onto the lightest fabric, you can be confident about using them without prewashing.

Fabric Grain. Fabrics are woven with threads going in a crosswise and lengthwise direction. The threads cross at right angles—the more threads per inch, the stronger the fabric.

The crosswise threads, or grain, have a small amount of give to them—they will stretch a little. The lengthwise threads will not stretch at all. Cutting the fabric at a 45-degree angle to the crosswise and lengthwise threads produces a bias edge which stretches a great deal when pulled (Figure 1). Bias strips are used when a lot of stretch is needed, such as for binding curved edges, stems for flowers or some appliqué shapes.

Pay careful attention to the grain lines marked with arrows on the templates given with the patterns, when marked. These arrows indicate

that the piece should be placed on the lengthwise grain with the arrow running on one thread. Although it is not necessary to examine the fabric and find a thread to match to, it is important to try to place the arrow with the lengthwise grain of the fabric (Figure 2).

Thread

One thing is for sure, Grandmother never had the choice of threads that we have today. For most piecing, good-quality cotton or cotton-covered polyester is the thread of choice. Inexpensive polyester threads are not recommended because they can cut the fibers of cotton fabrics. Choose a color thread that will match or blend with the fabrics in your quilt.

The same threads used for piecing can be used for quilting, but they will need to be waxed to keep them from tangling when quilting. Special quilting threads may be purchased in a variety of colors.

Batting

Batting is the material used to give a quilt loft or thickness and warmth. Warmth is determined by fiber thickness and type. For example, down feathers hold more air longer and are excellent insulators. Wool, silk and cotton are other good insulators. Our grandmothers used blankets, flannel or a purchased cotton or wool batting for their quilts. Polyester was not yet available. Today, quiltmakers are fortunate to have more choices.

Cotton battings are drapeable and fairly easy to quilt; they are also warm. Bearding, the migration of batt fibers to the outside layers of fabric, is not a problem. Cotton batting requires closer quilting lines (1/2" apart or closer) to prevent bunching and lumping, especially after laundering.

Cotton-blended batting combines the good qualities of cotton with the easy-care qualities of polyester. It is easy to work with and produces a thin-layered, warm quilt.

If you like to work with natural fibers, you may want to select wool or silk batting.

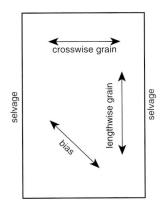

Figure 1
Drawing shows lengthwise, crosswise and bias threads.

crosswise grain

selvage

lengthwise grain

selvage

bias

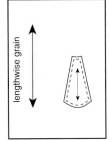

Figure 2
Place the template with marked arrow on the lengthwise grain of the fabric.

lengthwise grain

However, both are much more expensive than cotton or polyester batting, and silk is not widely available. Wool is a joy to work with, soft and easy to handle. Silk batting requires special techniques, so be sure to learn about it before you decide to work with it.

Polyester batting is inexpensive, easy to quilt and care for and is non-allergenic. Because of the bonding or glazing process, quilting lines can be farther apart. Polyester does have a tendency to beard.

To choose the right batting, determine how you plan to use the quilt and your method of quilting. If a quilt will receive frequent use, such as a child's quilt, the batting should be sturdy and washable. Consider a different batting if you are making a wall hanging, which will probably never be laundered. Thinner batts are easier to quilt by hand. In machine quilting a thick batt is not a problem.

Batting can be purchased by the yard in different widths or by the package ranging in size from craft size (36" x 45") to king size (120" x 120"). The patterns in this book give the size of the finished quilt; purchase a batting size that can be cut a little larger than these measurements. The excess will be trimmed away prior to binding the quilt.

Tools & Equipment

There are few truly essential tools and little equipment required for quiltmaking. The basics include needles (hand-sewing and quilting betweens), pins (long, thin sharp pins are best), sharp scissors or shears, a thimble, template materials (plastic or cardboard), marking tools (chalk marker, water-erasable pen and a No. 2 pencil are a few) and a quilting frame or hoop. For piecing and/or quilting by machine, add a sewing machine to the list.

Other sewing basics such as a seam ripper, pincushion, measuring tape and an iron are also necessary. In choosing colors or quilting designs for your quilt, or for designing your own quilt, it is helpful to have on hand graph paper, tracing paper, colored pencils or markers and a ruler.

There are many non-essential quilting gadgets on the market today. Items such as rotary cutters and mats, specialty rulers and bias bars can be fun to use and can make quiltmaking faster and easier.

As you become more involved in quiltmaking, your collection of tools will grow. Comfort, convenience and budget will determine your choices. Choose the best tools you can afford that will allow you to do your best work.

Techniques

Templates are like the pattern pieces used to sew a garment. They are used to cut the fabric pieces which make up the quilt top. There are two types—templates that include a 1/4" seam allowance and those that don't. In quiltmaking, the standard seam allowance is 1/4".
Note: *All measurements given in this book are the cut size and include the 1/4" seam allowance unless otherwise directed.*

Making Templates

Choose the template material and the pattern. Transfer the pattern shapes to the template material with a sharp No. 2 lead pencil. Write the pattern name, piece letter or number, grain line and number to cut for one block (whole quilt) on each piece. For hand-piecing, some quiltmakers prefer not to include the seam allowance on the template.

To make templates for hand-piecing, use the dotted sewing line as the guide for cutting templates.

Trace each template onto the backside or wrong side of the fabric, leaving 1/2" between shapes to allow for seams when cutting. The traced line is the stitching line (instructions for stitching will follow).

For machine piecing, make templates using the pattern pieces given. Cut the template accurately on the marked line and check it against the printed pattern when finished.

Some patterns require a reversed piece (Figure 3). These patterns are labeled with an R after the piece letter—for example, B and BR. To reverse a template, first cut it with the labeled side up and then with the labeled side down. Compare these to the right and left fronts of a blouse. When making a garment, you accomplish reversed pieces when cutting the pattern on two layers of fabric placed with right sides together. This can be done when cutting templates as well.

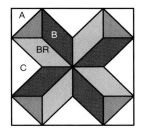

Figure 3
This pattern uses reversed pieces.

To make accurate templates when cutting more than one layer, iron the two layers of fabric with right sides together. Pin every 6" to hold before tracing templates onto the fabric.

If cutting one layer of fabric at a time, first trace the template onto the backside of the fabric with the marked side down; turn the template over with the marked side on the top to make reverse pieces.

Appliqué patterns given in this book do not include a seam allowance. Most designs are given in one drawing rather than individual pieces. This saves space while giving you the complete design to trace on the background block to help with placement of the pieces later. Make templates for each shape using the drawing for exact size. Remember to label each piece as for piecing templates.

For hand appliqué, add a seam allowance when cutting pieces from fabric. You may trace the template with label side up on the right side of the fabric if you are careful to mark lightly. The traced line is then the guide for turning the edges under when stitching.

If you prefer to mark on the wrong side of the fabric, turn the template over so the pattern faces the same way it does on the page.

For machine appliqué, a seam allowance is not necessary. Trace template onto the right side of the fabric with label facing up. Cut around shape on the traced line.

Piecing

Most of our grandmothers hand-pieced their quilts. Many quilters today still prefer hand piecing over machine piecing because it is portable and accurate. It is also very relaxing.

Hand-Piecing Basics. When hand-piecing it is easier to begin with templates which do not include the 1/4" seam allowance. Place the template on the wrong side of the fabric, lining up the marked grain line with lengthwise or crosswise fabric grain. If the piece does not have to be reversed, place with labeled side up. Trace around shape; move, leaving 1/2" between the shapes, and mark again.

When you have marked the appropriate number of pieces, cut out pieces, leaving 1/4" beyond marked line all around each piece. Some people are comfortable eyeballing this 1/4" while for others measuring and marking this line is easier.

Pieced patterns in this book include a drawing suggesting the assembly order. Refer to these drawings to piece units which are joined with other units to make rows. Finally the rows are joined to finish the blocks.

To join two units, place the patches with right sides together. Stick a pin in at the beginning of the seam through both fabric patches, matching the beginning points (Figure 4); for hand-piecing, the seam begins on the traced line, not at the edge of the fabric (Figure 5).

Figure 4
Stick a pin through fabrics to match the beginning of the seam.

Figure 5
Begin hand-piecing at seam, not at the edge of the fabric. Continue stitching along seam line.

Thread a sharp needle and knot one strand of the thread at the end. Remove the pin and insert the needle in the hole; make a short stitch and then a backstitch right over the first stitch. Continue making short stitches with several stitches on the needle at one time. As you stitch, check the back piece often to assure accurate stitching on the seam line. Take a stitch at the end of the seam; backstitch and knot at the same time as shown in Figure 6.

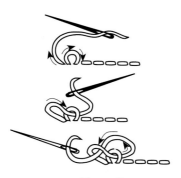

Figure 6
Make a loop in a backstitch to make a knot.

Seams on hand-pieced fabric patches may be finger-pressed toward the darker fabric.

To sew units together, pin fabric patches together, matching seams. Sew as above except where seams meet; at these intersections, backstitch, go through the seam to the next piece and backstitch again to secure seam joint.

Not all pieced blocks can be stitched with straight seams or in rows. Some pieces must be set into angled openings. Setting the corner

squares into the diamond-shaped openings of the *Lone Star* quilt on Page 77 requires exact stitching to insert the square at the right angle.

Pin one side of the square to the proper side of the star point with right sides together, matching corners. Start stitching at the seam line on the outside point; stitch on the marked seam line to the end of the seam line at the center referring to Figure 7.

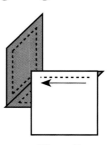

Figure 7
To set a square into a diamond point, match seams and stitch from outside edge to center.

Bring around the adjacent side and pin to the next star point, matching seams. Continue the stitching line from the adjacent seam through corners and to the outside edge of the square as shown in Figure 8.

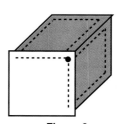

Figure 8
Continue stitching the adjacent side of the square to the next diamond shape in 1 seam from center to outside as shown.

Continue stitching the adjacent side of the square to the next diamond shape in one seam from center to outside as shown.

Machine-Piecing Blocks. Make templates including 1/4" seam allowance as given with each quilt pattern. Place template on the wrong side of the fabric as for hand-piecing except butt pieces against one another when tracing.

Join pieces as for hand-piecing for set-in seams; but for other straight seams, begin and end sewing at the end of the fabric patch sewn as shown in Figure 9.

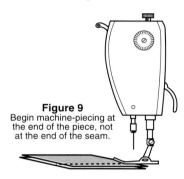

Figure 9
Begin machine-piecing at
the end of the piece, not
at the end of the seam.

Join units as for hand-piecing referring to the piecing diagrams given with each pattern. Chain piecing (Figure 10—sewing several like units before sewing other units) saves time by eliminating beginning and ending stitches.

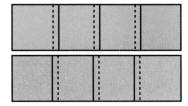

Figure 10
Units may be
chain-pieced to
save time.

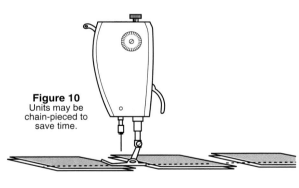

Figure 11
Sew machine-pieced units with seams
pressed in opposite directions.

When joining machine-pieced units, match seams against each other with seam allowances pressed in opposite directions to reduce bulk and make perfect matching of seams possible (Figure 11).

If pieces do not fit together perfectly, sometimes it is possible to ease the fabric pieces while keeping the seams matching.

Whether hand- or machine-piecing, check blocks when completed for correct size. If possible, try to trim all matching blocks to the same size. If sewing and cutting have been accurate, all blocks should be the same size without trimming.

Quick-Cutting & Piecing. Many quiltmakers prefer to use a rotary cutter, ruler and mat to cut fabric pieces with straight edges. This can be done on multiple layers, saving a great deal of time. Accuracy is very important when using these methods just as it is when you cut each piece individually.

When the pattern piece required is a square, it is a simple matter to fold the fabric, straighten the edge to be cut, lay the ruler on the fabric edge on the line corresponding to the size of the square and cut across the fabric with a rotary cutter. The resulting strip is then cut into the same increment. For example if you need a 2" square, cut a 2" strip across the width of the fabric. Cut that strip into 2" segments to make the squares (Figure 12). This will work for any size square.

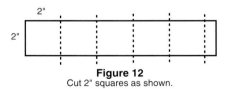

Figure 12
Cut 2" squares as shown.

If you need triangles, you can use the same method, but you need to figure out how wide to cut the strip. Measure the finished size of one side of the triangle. Add 7/8" to this size for seam allowance. Cut fabric strips this width; cut the strips into the same increment to create squares. Cut the squares on the diagonal to produce triangles. For example, if you need a triangle with a 2" finished height, cut the strips 2 7/8" by the width of the fabric. Cut the strips into 2 7/8" squares. Cut each square on the diagonal to produce the correct-size triangle (Figure 13).

Figure 13
Cut 2" (finished size) triangles from 2 7/8"
squares as shown.

Triangles sewn together to make squares are called half-square triangles or triangle/squares. When squares are cut on the diagonal to make these triangles, the straight of grain is on the two short sides, not the diagonal. When joined, the triangle/square unit has the straight of grain on all outside edges of the block.

Half-square triangles are used to make many designs. See the *Pinwheel Baby Quilt* on Page 21 for an example of a quilt that could be made using these quick methods instead of templates.

If you need triangles with the straight of grain on the diagonal, such as for fill-in triangles on the outside edges of a diagonal-set quilt (see *Patience Corner* on Page 143 for example), the procedure is a bit different.

To make these triangles, a square is cut on both diagonals; thus, the straight of grain is on the longest, or diagonal, side (Figure 14). To figure out the size to cut the square, add 1 1/4" to the needed finished size of the longest side of the triangle. For example, if you need a triangle with a 12" finished diagonal, cut a 13 1/4" square.

Because our grandmothers did not use these faster methods and modern tools, the patterns in this book are mainly focused on traditional methods. However, any of the templates may be cut using faster methods.

Figure 14
Add 1 1/4" to the finished size of the longest side
of the triangle needed and cut on both diagonals
to make a quarter-square triangle.

Appliqué

Appliqué is the process of applying one piece of fabric on top of another for decorative or functional purposes. As a functional technique appliqué is used to patch or cover a damaged portion of a garment or other fabric covering. Decoratively, appliqué is used creatively on clothing, wall hangings and quilts.

Making Templates. Most appliqué designs given here are not broken down into individual pieces, but are given as full-size drawings for the completed designs. The drawings show dotted lines to indicate where one piece overlaps another. Other marks indicate placement of embroidery stitches for decorative purposes such as eyes, lips, flowers, etc.

For hand appliqué, trace each template onto the right side of the fabric with template right side up. Be sure the traced line is light but dark enough to see. Cut around shape, adding a 1/8"–1/4" seam allowance.

Before the actual appliqué process begins, cut the background block and prepare it for stitching. Most appliqué designs are centered on the block. To find the center of the background square, fold it in half and in half again and crease with your fingers. Now unfold and fold diagonally and crease; repeat for other corners referring to Figure 15.

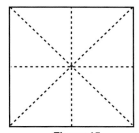

Figure 15
Fold background to mark centers as shown.

You now have a block with center-line creases to help position the design. If centering the appliqué design is important, an X has been placed on each drawing to mark the center of the design. This X may be matched with the creased center of the background block when placing pieces. If you have a full-size drawing of the design, as is given with most appliqué designs in this book, it might help you to draw the design on the background block to help with placement.

First transfer the design to a large piece of paper—tracing paper would be the easiest kind to use. Place the paper on top of the design; use masking tape to hold in place. Trace design onto paper.

If you have a light box, the next step is easy. Many people do not have one of these helpful devices. Inventive quilters have found that a large window works almost as well if you can stand up close. Tape the pattern on the window; center the background block on top and tape in place. Trace the design onto the background block with a water-erasable marker or chalk pencil. This drawing will mark exactly where the fabric pieces should be placed on the background block.

There are several methods of appliqué. Some projects would be easier to hand-appliqué, while machine appliqué is appropriate for others. Choose the method that works best for you and for the quilt you have chosen.

Hand Appliqué. Our grandmothers most often used the traditional hand-appliqué method. The preferred method is to use a template made from the desired finished shape without seam allowance added. Fabrics are chosen (100 percent cotton is recommended) and prepared as instructed on Page 152.

When fabric is prepared and ironed, trace the desired shape onto the right side of the fabric with a water-erasable marker, light lead or chalk pencil. Leave at least 1/2" between design motifs when tracing to allow for the seam allowance when cutting out the shapes.

When the desired number of shapes needed has been drawn on the fabric pieces, cut out shapes leaving 1/8"–1/4" all around drawn line for turning under.

Some appliqué experts recommend stitching around the shape just outside the turning line to provide a guide for turning. This keeps the piece from stretching out of shape as you work with it. It is an optional step but one you might like to try.

Turn the shape's edges over on the drawn or stitched line. When turning the edges under, remember to make sharp corners sharp and smooth edges smooth. Smooth edges should not have points and pointed edges should not be rounded. The fabric patch should retain the shape of the template used to cut it.

Basting the edges over may be helpful to some stitchers. When the edges are basted over before the actual appliqué process, the shape is already formed. This helps to make the process easier for some people. Other stitchers prefer to turn the edge under with a needle as they work rather than take the time necessary for hand-basting.

When turning in concave curves, clip to seams

and baste the seam allowance over as shown in Figure 16.

Figure 16
Concave curves should be clipped
before turning as shown.

During the actual appliqué process, you may be layering one shape on top of another. Where two fabrics overlap, the underneath piece does not have to be turned under or stitched down.

If possible, the underneath fabric should be trimmed away when the block is finished. This is accomplished by carefully cutting away the background from underneath and then cutting away unnecessary layers. Quilting through several layers by machine is not a problem, but hand-quilting through many layers is not an easy process.

Sometimes the top layer is a lighter fabric than the next layer and the darker fabric shadows through to the top. Cutting away the underneath layer in this case removes the shadowing layer.

Position the fabric shapes on the background block and pin or baste them in place. Using a blind stitch or appliqué stitch, sew pieces in place with matching thread and small stitches. Start with background pieces first and work up to foreground pieces. Patterns in this book are numbered. Appliqué the pieces in place on the background in numerical order, layering as necessary.

Machine Appliqué. Machine appliqué can be as beautiful as hand appliqué. Good machine appliqué is not easy to accomplish. There are several products available to help make the process easier and faster.

Some stitchers advocate the use of a fusible transfer web product. Fusible transfer web is similar to iron-on interfacings except it has two sticky sides. Paper is adhered to one side.

To use, dry-iron the sticky side of the fusible product onto the wrong side of the chosen fabric. Draw desired shapes onto the paper and cut them out. Peel off the paper and dry-iron the shapes in place on the background fabric. The shape will stay in place while you stitch around it. This process adds a little bulk or stiffness to the appliquéd shape and makes quilting through the layers by hand difficult.

Another product that helps make machine appliqué easier is a tear-off stabilizer. This product is placed under the background fabric while machine appliqué is being done. It is torn away when the work is finished. This kind of stabilizer keeps the background fabric from pulling during the machine-appliqué process.

During the actual machine-appliqué process, you will be layering one shape on top of another. Where two fabrics overlap, the underneath piece does not have to be turned under or stitched down.

Thread the top of the machine with thread to match the fabric patches or with threads that coordinate or contrast with fabrics. Rayon thread is a good choice when a sheen is desired on the finished appliqué stitches. Do not use rayon thread in the bobbin; use all-purpose thread.

Set your machine to make a zigzag stitch and practice on scraps of similar weight to check the tension. If you can see the bobbin thread on the top of the appliqué, adjust your machine to make a balanced stitch. Different-width stitches are available; choose one that will not overpower the appliqué shapes. In some cases these appliqué stitches will be used as decorative stitches as well and you may want the thread to show.

If using a stabilizer, place this under the background fabric and pin or fuse in place. Place shapes as for hand-appliqué and stitch all around shapes by machine.

When all machine work is complete, remove stabilizer from the back referring to the manufacturer's instructions.

Making Bias Strips for Appliqué. Cut bias strips twice the needed width plus the seam allowance. For example, if you need a bias strip for a 1/2"-wide stem, cut strips 1 1/2" wide. Fold the strips wrong sides together lengthwise and stitch along seam allowance.

Slip a 1/2" bias bar inside the strip, centering the seam on the back of the strip. Press with bar inside the strip. Remove the bias bar and

Appliqué Stitches

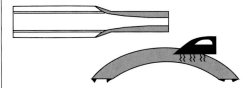

Stems: Stem pieces for flowers and leaves are usually cut on the fabric's bias or diagonal grain. This helps them to curve easily. There are special tools that can help you make your bias strips, or you may purchase pre-made bias tape. It is not always available in the colors you need. If you have no tools available, you might make a cardboard template in the required finished width, fold the fabric around it and press in place. Press and place on fabric.

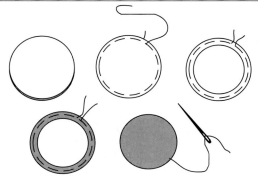

Circles: Cut a cardboard template the size of the finished circle. Sew a basting stitch around fabric piece on seam line. Place fabric piece centered over template and pull basting stitches to gather piece around cardboard shape. Press gently with iron and pull out template. Sew in place.

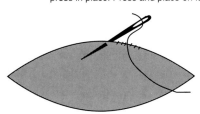

Appliqué Stitch: Use a close slipstitch or blind stitch to secure the pieces to the background.

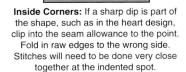

Pointed Corners: Clip off seam allowance to 1/8" below point. Fold point over at tip to seam allowance. Fold in trimmed sides at seam line. This method is most commonly needed when appliquéing leaves.

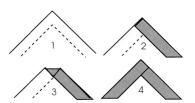

Corners: To make a neat square corner, fold in 1 edge of the piece 1/4" or on seam line to the wrong side; then fold over second edge. For corners that have very pointed edges, such as a leaf, fold down tip first, then fold in sides. Excess fabric might need to be trimmed.

Inside Corners: If a sharp dip is part of the shape, such as in the heart design, clip into the seam allowance to the point. Fold in raw edges to the wrong side. Stitches will need to be done very close together at the indented spot.

Curved Edges: Difficult curved edges are easy to work with by using the needle to turn the seam allowance under as you stitch.

you will have a perfect bias stem.

If you don't have a bias bar, cut strips the width needed, plus a seam allowance. Fold over one edge and press. Place on background block and appliqué in place. Flatten down with fingers and turn under other edge as you stitch it in place using the tip of the needle.

Embellishments. To add dimension to the pieces, a bit of stuffing may be inserted in a piece before the final stitches are made. This technique is called trapunto. Be sure that the stuffing is distributed evenly before final stitches are made. Do not cut away background fabric from beneath stuffed areas.

Several of the appliqué patterns given in this book require some added detail work with embroidery stitches. Many shapes are too small to be appliquéd but are integral parts of the design. These shapes are added with embroidery stitches and floss.

In some cases, these details can be eliminated, if you prefer not to add them; however, these little details add a great deal to the finished

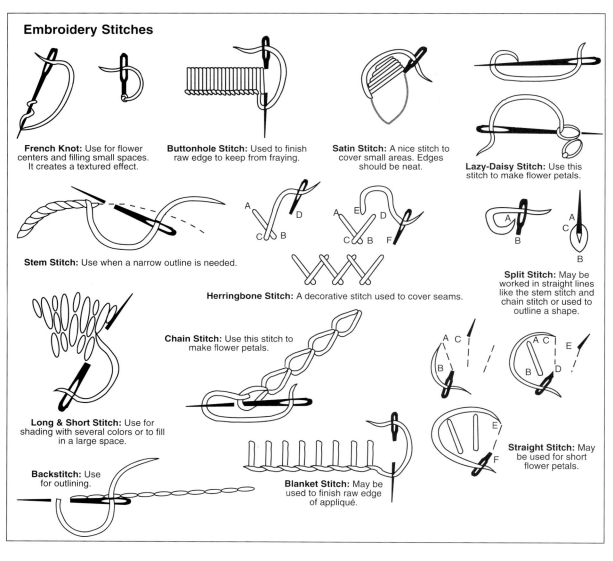

Embroidery Stitches

French Knot: Use for flower centers and filling small spaces. It creates a textured effect.

Buttonhole Stitch: Used to finish raw edge to keep from fraying.

Satin Stitch: A nice stitch to cover small areas. Edges should be neat.

Lazy-Daisy Stitch: Use this stitch to make flower petals.

Stem Stitch: Use when a narrow outline is needed.

Herringbone Stitch: A decorative stitch used to cover seams.

Split Stitch: May be worked in straight lines like the stem stitch and chain stitch or used to outline a shape.

Chain Stitch: Use this stitch to make flower petals.

Long & Short Stitch: Use for shading with several colors or to fill in a large space.

Straight Stitch: May be used for short flower petals.

Backstitch: Use for outlining.

Blanket Stitch: May be used to finish raw edge of appliqué.

look of the blocks. Diagrams of the most common stitches are given here. Color and stitches used may be chosen to suit your own stitching tastes.

Special shapes require special skills and the diagrams shown provide some extra help in successful completion of appliqué of these shapes. Try every method to see which one you prefer. If appliqué is new to you, practice applying shapes to a background block using one or all of the methods given here. Choose the method that works best for you, or invent one of your own!

Putting It All Together

If your quilt is made up of individual blocks, they must be set together somehow to make them into a quilt top. The instructions accompanying the quilts in this book tell you how to do this, but you might like to change the setting. You have several choices.

Settings

Sometimes the choices are limited by the block's design. For example, a house block should be placed upright on a quilt, not sideways or upside down.

A straight setting where blocks are joined in rows block-to-block against one another is the easiest. Sometimes when pieced blocks are joined in this way, alternate designs are formed where the pieces on the edge of the blocks meet, as is evidenced by the *Hearts & Gizzards* pattern on Page 115. It is necessary to match seams carefully when sewing blocks together in this way (Figure 17).

Figure 17
Butt the blocks against one another and sew in rows. Alternate designs are formed when blocks are pieced this way.

Plain blocks can be alternated with pieced or appliquéd blocks in a straight set (Figure 18). Making a quilt using plain blocks saves time; half the number of pieced or appliquéd blocks are needed to make the same-size quilt. If you like to show off your quilting stitches with pretty uninterrupted designs, these solid blocks are a wonderful place to do that. (See *Razz-Ma-Tazz* on Page 13.)

Another common setting method is framing the blocks with sashing or lattice strips (Figure 19). These strips are cut the length of the block plus seams and a width that is in scale with the blocks. For example, a good sashing strip size for a 12" block is 3".

Figure 18
Alternate plain blocks with pieced blocks to save time making more pieced or appliquéd blocks.

Figure 19
Blocks may be joined with sashing strips.

The blocks are joined in rows with the strips. Longer strips are cut to join the rows, or sashing squares are placed at the junction of the

Figure 20
Sashing squares may be added as shown.

seams to break up the design and add a contrast to the sashing-strip colors (Figure 20). The *Scrappy Triangles* quilt on Page 17 uses short and long sashing strips to join the blocks.

Blocks may be joined with pieced strips. This type of quilt takes a bit more time; the investment in time is worth the effort when the quilt is complete. The *Antique Sunflower Quilt* on Page 119 uses a *Flying Geese* unit set in rows to separate the pieced blocks.

Quilt blocks may be set together on the diagonal. When this method is used, corner and side fill-in triangles are needed to square up the quilt top as shown in Figure 21. These triangles may be cut using the methods described on Page 158.

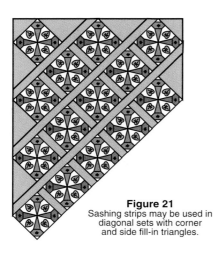

Figure 21
Sashing strips may be used in
diagonal sets with corner
and side fill-in triangles.

In a diagonal set, the rows are stitched together on the diagonal and then joined. Sashing squares and lattice strips may be added to diagonal sets in the same way they are in straight sets as shown in Figure 22 and in the *Grandmother's Square in a Square* quilt on Page 37.

Some quilts are set on the diagonal and use portions of the blocks to square up the quilt. In this type of quilt, the pieced sections of the quilt are not simply cut from completed blocks; they require different templates to create that portion of the block. The *Flower Basket* quilt top on Page 25 uses this setting method.

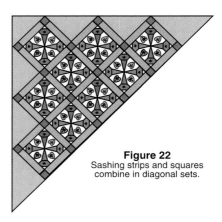

Figure 22
Sashing strips and squares
combine in diagonal sets.

Adding Borders

Borders should not be added to a quilt top on a whim. They are an integral part of the quilt and should complement the colors and designs used in the quilt center. Borders frame a quilt just like a mat and frame do a picture. Borders can be fancy or plain, but they should relate to the fabrics and designs used in the quilt center.

Border strips may be mitered at the corners or butted as shown in Figures 23 and 24. To find out the size for butted border strips, measure across center of the completed quilt top from one side raw edge to the other side raw edge (Figure 25). This measurement will include a 1/4" seam allowance. Cut two border strips that length by the chosen width of the border. Sew these strips to the top and bottom of the pieced center (Figure 26). Press the seam allowance toward border strips.

Measure across the completed quilt top at the center, from top raw edge to bottom raw edge, including the two border strips added. Cut two border strips that length by the chosen width of the border. Sew a strip to the two remaining sides (Figure 27). Press the seams toward border strips.

Carefully press the entire piece, including the pieced center. Avoid pulling and stretching while pressing, which would distort shapes.

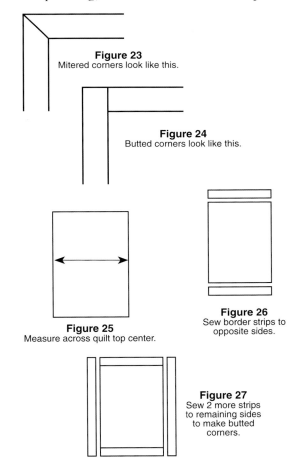

Figure 23
Mitered corners look like this.

Figure 24
Butted corners look like this.

Figure 25
Measure across quilt top center.

Figure 26
Sew border strips to opposite sides.

Figure 27
Sew 2 more strips to remaining sides to make butted corners.

To make mitered corners, measure the quilt as before. Double the width of the border and add seam allowance to determine the length of the strips. Repeat for opposite sides. Sew on each strip, stopping stitching 1/4" from corner, leaving the remainder of the strip dangling.

Sew on all four strips. Press corners at a 45-degree angle to form a crease. Stitch from the inside quilt corner to the outside on the creased line. Trim excess away after stitching and press mitered seams open (Figures 28–30).

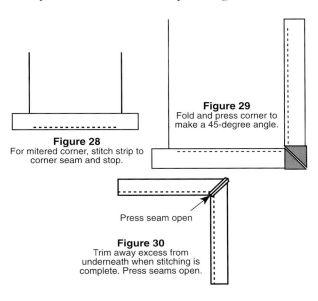

Figure 28
For mitered corner, stitch strip to corner seam and stop.

Figure 29
Fold and press corner to make a 45-degree angle.

Press seam open

Figure 30
Trim away excess from underneath when stitching is complete. Press seams open.

Quilting Designs & Techniques

If you choose to hand- or machine-quilt your finished top, you will need to choose a design for quilting.

Choosing a Quilting Design. Manufactured quilt-design templates are available in many designs and sizes. These templates are inexpensive and worth the investment if you can find a design you like. The design is cut out of a durable plastic template material and is easy to use.

There are several types of quilting designs, some of which may not have to be marked. The easiest of the unmarked designs is in-the-ditch quilting. With this method, the quilting stitches are placed in the valley created by the seams joining two pieces together or next to the edge of an appliqué design. There is no need to mark a top for in-the-ditch quilting.

Many machine quilters choose this option because the stitches are not as obvious on the finished quilt (Figure 31).

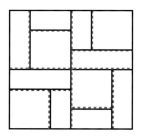

Figure 31
In-the-ditch quilting is done in the
seam that joins 2 pieces.

Outline-quilting 1/4" or more away from seams or appliqué shapes is another no-mark alternative (Figure 32). When outline quilting, one avoids having to sew through the layers made by seams, thus making stitching easier.

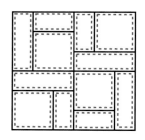

Figure 32
Outline-quilting 1/4" away from
seam is a popular choice for quilting.

Some stitchers may have to mark the quilting lines for outline quilting, while others are very good at eyeballing the 1/4" (or other distance). Masking tape is available in different widths and is helpful to place on straight-edge designs to mark the quilting line. If using masking tape, place the tape right up against the seam and quilt close to the other edge.

Appliqué shapes may be outline-quilted. If more than one row of outline stitches is used, it is called echo-quilting. Evenly space the echo-quilting rows around the design and continue to create the design in subsequent rows (Figure 33).

Figure 33
Echo quilting repeats the design. It is often used
when quilting appliqué quilts.

Sometimes the quilting is done in the background around an appliqué shape. An example of this is cross-hatch quilting where straight lines cross each other at 90-degree angles on the background but do not go through the appliqué shapes as shown in Figure 34.

Figure 34
Cross-hatch quilting is done on
the background.

Other designs, such as the clamshell pattern, are quilted in an allover design with no regard to the pieced or appliquéd design as shown in

Figure 35. Many commercial quilting machines use this type of design.

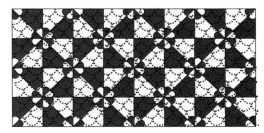

Figure 35
The allover clamshell quilting design is stitched over the entire quilt top with no regard to the quilt's pattern.

Marking the Top for Quilting or Tying. If you choose a fancy or allover design for quilting, you will need to transfer the design to your quilt top.

There are several methods from which to choose for marking. Each one may work better for one project than another due to differences in fabrics or colors used on your quilt top. Experiment on scraps before actually trying any of these on your finished top.

The chosen quilting design should be marked on the quilt top before layering with the backing and batting. It is easier to lay the quilt flat and mark lines without the batting layer to distort the design.

Just as in all other areas of quilting, there are exceptions. Some quilters prefer to mark small areas at a time. If you will be using a frame or a hoop where your top will be held taut, it is possible to mark the quilting design on as you stitch. Generally speaking, though, the quilting design is marked on the top before layering with backing and batting.

A sharp medium-lead pencil may be used on light background fabrics. Test the pencil marks

to guarantee that they will wash out of your quilt top when quilting is complete; or be sure your quilting stitches cover the pencil marks. Mechanical pencils with very fine points may be used successfully to mark quilts.

Many quilters have discovered that a silver pencil works well for marking quilting designs on quilt tops. Many quilt shops carry these pencils so you won't have to buy a set of colored pencils just to get one color!

Our grandmothers used soap slivers to mark designs on dark fabrics. Of course, we know soap will wash out so there is no danger of leaving a mark on a finished quilt top.

No matter what marking method you use, remember—the marked lines should never show on the finished quilt. When the top is marked, it is ready for layering.

Preparing the Quilt Backing. The quilt backing is a very important feature of your quilt. In most cases, the Materials list for each quilt in this book gives the size requirements for the backing, not the yardage needed. Exceptions to this are when the backing fabric is also used on the quilt top and yardage is given for that fabric.

A backing is generally cut at least 4" larger than the quilt top or 2" larger on all sides. For a 64" x 78" finished quilt, the backing would need to be at least 68" x 82".

Fabrics used in quilting are almost always 45" wide; therefore, more than one width of fabric is needed for the backing. There are several ways to create the backing piece in the required size. The easiest way to seam the fabrics would be to sew two correct-length pieces together along one lengthwise seam; however, this is not the best way.

Avoid having the seam across the center of the quilt backing. A better alternative is to cut or tear one of the correct-length pieces in half and sew half to each side of the second piece (Figures 36 and 37).

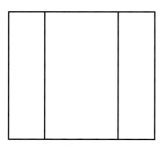

Figure 36
Center 1 backing piece
with a piece on each side.

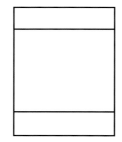

Figure 37
Horizontal seams may be
used on backing pieces.

Some quilters like to be creative with their backing pieces. They combine large fabric pieces with pieced blocks or similar segments used on the top. Being creative with the backing makes an interesting quilt. Although not many of our grandmothers used this method, we do have one example showing crazy-pieced strips being used for a backing (see *Pinwheel Baby Quilt,* Page 21).

If you are not confident you will make good quilting stitches on the back of your quilt, use a print fabric. It will hide your stitches better than a solid fabric. Choose a fabric that will not show through the batting to the front of your quilt top. For example, do not use black backing on a quilt with a white top.

Take some time to consider your backing. It is a very important part of your finished quilt. It should lie flat and straight. Choosing plaids or stripes will make it almost impossible to hide a crooked side; avoid these fabrics for backings. Try to line the straight of grain of the backing up with the edges of the quilt top to avoid stretching during the quilting process.

Choose the best quality backing fabric you can afford—one with the same fiber content and weave as the fabrics used on the quilt top. Although bed sheets have often been used as backings because they come as one piece in a variety of sizes, be careful about using them. The thread count in a good sheet is very high which makes it difficult to quilt through.

Layering the Quilt Sandwich. Layering the quilt top with the batting and backing is a time-consuming process. If you have access to a large open area with big tables such as at a church or school, it makes the process a bit easier. A group of friends to help can make the work go faster and be more fun.

Begin with getting the batting to lie flat. It helps to open it up several days before you need it. It could be placed over a bed or flat on the floor to help flatten the creases caused from its being folded up in the bag for such a long time.

Iron the backing piece, folding in half both vertically and horizontally and pressing. These lines mark the centers, which should be matched to the centers on the quilt top during the layering process.

If you will not be quilting on a frame, place the backing right side down on a clean floor or tables. Start in the center and push any wrinkles or bunches flat. Use masking tape to tape the edges to the floor or large clips to hold the backing to the edge of the tables. The backing should be taut.

Place the batting on top of the backing, matching centers using fold lines as guides; flatten out any wrinkles. Trim the batting to the same size as the backing.

Fold the quilt top in half lengthwise and place on top of the batting, wrong side against the batting, matching centers. Unfold quilt and, working from the center to the outside edges, smooth out any wrinkles or lumps.

To hold the quilt layers together for quilting, baste by hand or use safety pins. If basting by hand, thread a long thin needle with a long piece of white or off-white thread. Do not knot the thread. Starting in the center and leaving a long tail, make 4"–6" stitches toward one outside edge of the quilt top, smoothing as you baste. Start at the center again and work toward the outside in another direction.

If quilting by machine, you may prefer to use

safety pins for holding your fabric sandwich together. Start in the center of the quilt and pin to the outside, leaving pins open until all are placed. When you are satisfied that all layers are smooth, close the pins.

Some quilting frames do not require basting the layers together for quilting; rather, the backing is placed on a separate roller than the top and batting and the layers are kept taut for quilting by the frame. Read the instructions with your quilt frame before preparing your quilt top for quilting.

The layering process is very important to create a flat quilt without wrinkles on the top and bottom. Don't hurry the layering and basting processes just because they aren't fun—it can mean the difference between a neat, flat quilt or a lumpy one when you are finished.

Hand Quilting. Hand quilting is the process of placing stitches through the quilt top, batting and backing to hold them together. While it is a functional process, it also adds beauty and loft to the finished quilt. Because some quilts consist only of a plain top with a quilted design, quilting can be the focal point of many quilts.

To begin, thread a sharp between needle with an 18" piece of quilting thread. Tie a small knot in the end of the thread. Position the needle about 1/2"–1" away from the starting point on quilt top. Sink needle through the top into the batting layer but not through the backing. Pull the needle up at the starting point of the quilting design. Pull the needle and thread until the knot sinks through the top into the batting (Figure 38).

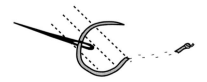

Figure 38
Start the needle through the top layer of fabric 1/2"–1"
away from quilting line with knot on top of fabric.

Some stitchers like to take a backstitch here at the beginning while others prefer to begin the first stitch here. Take small, even running stitches along the marked quilting line (Figure 39). Keep one hand positioned underneath to feel the needle go all the way through to the backing. The objective is to make stitches even on the back as well as on the front.

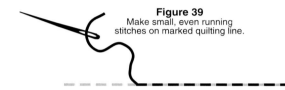

Figure 39
Make small, even running
stitches on marked quilting line.

When you have nearly run out of thread, wind the thread around the needle several times to make a small knot and pull it close to the fabric. Insert the needle into the fabric on the quilting line and come out with the needle 1/2"–1" away, pulling the knot into the fabric layers the same as when you started. Pull and cut thread close to fabric. The end should disappear inside after cutting. Some quilters prefer to take a backstitch with a loop through it for a knot to end.

You will perfect your quilting stitches as you gain experience. If you watch other quilters at work, you will realize that not many work in the same way. They have developed their own quilting style which works for them, but may not work for you. Don't be discouraged with your first attempts, especially if you are not an experienced needleworker to begin with. Your quilting stitches will get better with each project and your style will be uniquely your own.

Machine Quilting. Some quilters turn their nose up at machine quilting. This may be because they have never tried it. It is not easy. It takes practice and a good relationship with your sewing machine to find success. Do not attempt machine-quilting a full-size quilt without many hours of practice first.

Basically the quilt is prepared for quilting in the same way as for hand-quilting. Use safety pins to hold the layers together instead of basting with thread. Set the machine on a longer stitch length (three or eight to 10 stitches to the inch). Too tight a stitch causes puckering and fabric tucks, either on the quilt top or backing.

An even-feed or walking foot helps to eliminate the tucks and puckering by feeding the upper and lower layers through the machine evenly. Before you begin, loosen the amount of pressure on the presser foot.

Tied Quilts, or Comforters

Would you rather tie your quilt layers together than quilt them? Tied quilts are often referred to as comforters. The advantage of tying is that it takes so much less time and the required skills can be learned quickly.

If you will be tying your quilt top, choose a thick, bonded batting—one that will not separate during washing. For tying, use pearl cotton, embroidery floss or strong yarn in colors that match or coordinate with the fabrics in your quilt top.

Decide on a pattern for tying. Many quilts are tied at the corners and centers of the blocks and at sashing joints. Try to tie every 4"–6". Special designs can be used for tying, but most quilts are tied in conventional ways.

To make the tie, thread a large needle with a long thread (yarn, floss or crochet cotton); do not knot. Push the needle through the quilt top to the back, leaving a 3"–4" length on top. Move the needle to the next position without cutting thread. Take another stitch through the

Figure 40
Make a square knot as shown.

layers; repeat until thread is almost used up.

Cut thread between stitches, leaving an equal amount of thread on each stitch. Tie a knot with the two thread ends. Tie again to make a square knot referring to Figure 40. Trim thread ends to desired length.

Quilts may be tied on the back so as not to interfere with the design on the front. The same method is used, except that the tying design needs to be marked on the backing so that you will know where to make the ties.

Finishing the Edges

There is one way to eliminate adding an edge finish. This is done before quilting.

Without Binding, or Self-Finish

Place the backing right side down on a flat surface. Layer the batting on top of the wrong side of the backing. Place the pieced top right side down on the batting. Pin and/or baste the layers together to hold flat referring to Page 168.

Begin stitching in the center of one side using a 1/4" seam allowance, reversing at the beginning and end of the seam. Continue stitching all around and back to the beginning side. Leave a 12" or larger opening. Clip corners to reduce excess. Turn right side out through the opening.

Slipstitch the opening closed by hand. The quilt may now be quilted by hand or machine.

The disadvantage to this method is that once the edges are sewn in, any creases or wrinkles that might form during the quilting process cannot be flattened out. Tying is the preferred method of finishing a quilt constructed using this method.

Bringing the backing fabric to the front is another way to finish the quilt's edge without binding. To accomplish this, complete the quilt as for hand or machine quilting. Trim the batting *only* even with the front. Trim the backing 1" larger than the completed top all around.

Turn the backing edge in 1/2" and then turn

over to the front along edge of batting. The folded edge may be machine-stitched close to the edge through all layers, or blind-stitched in place to finish.

The front may be turned to the back. If using this method, a wider front border is needed. The backing and batting are trimmed 1" smaller than the top and the top edge is turned under 1/2" and then turned to the back and stitched in place.

One more method of self-finish may be used. The top and backing may be stitched together by hand at the edge. To accomplish this, all quilting must be stopped 1/2" from the quilt-top edge. The top and backing of the quilt are trimmed even and the batting is trimmed to 1/4"–1/2" smaller. The edges of the top and backing are turned in 1/4"–1/2" and blind-stitched together at the very edge.

These methods do not require the use of extra fabric and save time in preparation of binding strips. Remember that they are not as durable.

Binding

The technique of adding extra fabric at the edges of the quilt is called binding. The binding encloses the edges and adds an extra layer of fabric for durability.

To prepare the quilt for the addition of the binding, trim the batting and backing layers flush with the top of the quilt using a rotary cutter and ruler or shears. Using a walking-foot attachment (sometimes called an even-feed foot attachment), machine-baste the three layers together all around approximately 1/8" from the cut edge.

The list of materials given with each quilt in this book often includes a number of yards of self-made or purchased binding. Bias binding may be purchased in packages and in many colors. The advantage to self-made binding is that you can use fabrics from your quilt to coordinate colors.

Double-fold, straight-grain binding and double-fold, bias-grain binding are two of the most commonly used types of binding.

Double-fold, straight-grain binding is used on smaller projects with right-angle corners. Double-fold, bias-grain binding is best for bed-size quilts or quilts with rounded corners.

To make double-fold, straight-grain binding, cut 2"-wide strips of fabric across the width or down the length of the fabric totaling the perimeter of the quilt plus 10". The strips are joined as in Figure 41 and pressed in half wrong sides together along the length using

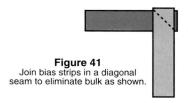

Figure 41
Join bias strips in a diagonal
seam to eliminate bulk as shown.

an iron on a cotton setting with no steam.

Lining up the raw edges, place the binding on the top of the quilt and begin sewing (again using the walking foot) approximately 6" from the beginning of the binding strip. Stop sewing 1/4" from the first corner and backstitch.

Turn the quilt; fold the binding at a 45-degree angle up and away from the quilt and back down flush with the raw edges. Starting at the top raw edge of the quilt, begin sewing the next side. Repeat at the next three corners as shown in Figures 42 and 43.

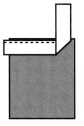

Figure 42
To make a mitered
corner on bound
edge, fold binding at a
45-degree seam to
eliminate bulk as
shown.

Figure 43
Fold the binding
strips back down,
flush with the raw
edge, and begin
sewing.

As you approach the beginning of the binding strip, stop stitching and overlap the binding 1/2" from the edge; trim. Join the two ends with a 1/4" seam allowance and press the seam open. Reposition the joined binding along the edge of the quilt and resume stitching to the beginning.

To finish, bring the folded edge of the binding over the raw edges and blind-stitch the binding in place over the machine-stitching line on the backside. Hand-miter the corners on the back as shown in Figure 44.

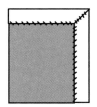

Figure 44
Miter and stitch corners as shown.

If you are making a quilt to be used on a bed, you will want to use double-fold, bias-grain bindings because the many threads that cross each other along the fold at the edge of the quilt make it a more durable binding.

Cut 2"-wide bias strips from a large square of fabric or use the method for making continuous bias that follows. Join the strips as illustrated in Figure 45 and press the seams open. Fold the beginning end of the bias strip 1/4" from the raw edge and press. Fold the joined strips in half along the long side, wrong sides together, and press with no steam (Figure 45).

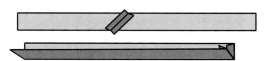

Figure 45
Fold end in and press strip in half.

Follow the same procedures as previously described for preparing the quilt top and sewing the binding to the quilt top. Remember, however, that bias strips have the ability to stretch a good deal so don't pull on the strip as you are attaching it. Treat the corners just as you treated them with straight-grain binding.

Since you are using bias-grain binding, you do have the option to just eliminate the corners if this option doesn't interfere with the patchwork in the quilt. This may be the answer for the quilter who gets cold sweats when she approaches the corner of her quilt with binding strips. You can round the corners off by placing one of your dinner plates at the corner and rotary-cutting the gentle curve (Figure 46).

Figure 46
Round corners to eliminate square-corner finishes.

As you approach the beginning of the bias strip, stop stitching and lay the end across the beginning so it will slip inside the fold. Cut the end at a 45-degree angle so the raw edges are contained inside the beginning of the strip (Figure 47). Resume stitching to the beginning. Bring the fold to the back of the quilt and hand-stitch as previously described.

Figure 47
End the binding strips as shown.

Overlapped corners are not quite as easy as rounded ones, but a bit easier than mitering. To make overlapped corners, sew binding strips to opposite sides of the quilt top. Stitch edges down to finish. Trim ends even.

Sew a strip to each remaining side, leaving 1 1/2"–2" excess at each end. Turn quilt over and fold binding down even with previous finished edge as shown in Figure 48.

Figure 48
Fold end of binding even with
previous edge.

Fold binding in toward quilt and stitch down as before, enclosing the previous bound edge in the seam. It may be necessary to trim the folded-down section to reduce bulk.

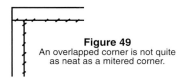

Figure 49
An overlapped corner is not quite
as neat as a mitered corner.

Making Continuous Bias Binding. Instead of cutting individual binding strips and sewing them together in one long strip, bias binding may be made in one continuous strip.

Begin with a square. To determine the size of the square needed, choose any size—for example, a 36" square. Multiply the length of one side by the length of another side. In this case, 36" times 36", or 1,296". Decide on the width of binding needed—for example, 2 1/2". Divide 1,296 by 2 1/2 to get the number of inches the square will produce, or 518.4". Divide that by 36 (the number of inches in a yard) to determine how many yards that is—14.4 yards. If you only need 10 yards of binding, a 36" square is too large—try another size.

After you determine the size square you need, cut a piece of fabric that size. Fold the square in half diagonally; press. Cut on the diagonal crease to make two triangles.

With right sides together, layer the triangles together as shown in Figure 50. Sew together 1/4" along edges. Open and press seam allowance open.

On the wrong side of the fabric, measure and mark parallel lines the desired width of the bias binding (in our case, 2 1/2") referring to Figure 51.

Now comes the tricky part: Fold the fabric with right sides together, lining up the bias edges but offsetting them by one width to make a tube referring to Figure 52. Pin and sew along edge using a 1/4" seam; press seam open.

Begin cutting on the line of the excess at the top of the tube referring to Figure 53. Continue cutting along the line until you come to the end. This creates one long strip of bias binding.

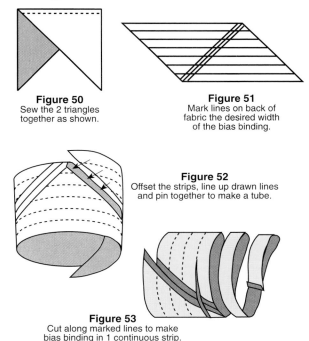

Figure 50
Sew the 2 triangles
together as shown.

Figure 51
Mark lines on back of
fabric the desired width
of the bias binding.

Figure 52
Offset the strips, line up drawn lines
and pin together to make a tube.

Figure 53
Cut along marked lines to make
bias binding in 1 continuous strip.

Prairie Points

Some quilts have triangles inserted at the edge (see *Mother's Handkerchiefs*, Page 147).

These triangles are called prairie points. To make prairie points, cut squares the size directed in the instructions given with the quilt or at least 3". Fold each triangle in half once and then in half again with wrong sides together as shown in Figure 54.

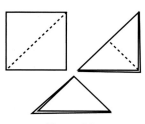

Figure 54
Fold squares for prairie
points as shown.

Place the resulting folded triangles at the edge of the quilt top, before the quilting process, with the raw edge of the triangle lined up with the quilt's edge. Overlap triangles one inside the other. Adjust the overlap to make the triangles fit the quilt's edge.

Machine-stitch in place 1/4" from edge of quilt as shown in Figure 55. Quilt the prepared quilt top as desired.

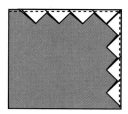

Figure 55
Machine-stitch the prairie
points in place.

When quilting is complete, trim layers even with the quilt top, then trim the batting an

additional 1/4". Turn the triangles toward the outside of the quilt's edge, which finishes the quilt top edges. Turn under the backing 1/4" and hand-stitch to triangles, enclosing the line of stitching holding the triangles together with the quilt top to finish (Figure 56).

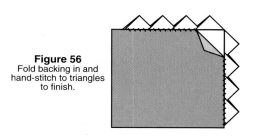

Figure 56
Fold backing in and
hand-stitch to triangles
to finish.

Final Touches

If your quilt will be hung on the wall, a hanging sleeve is required. Other options include purchased plastic rings or fabric tabs. The best choice is a fabric sleeve.

The sleeve will evenly distribute the weight of the quilt across the top edge rather than at selected spots where tabs or rings are stitched. This will keep the quilt hanging straight and not damage the batting.

To make a sleeve, measure across the top of the finished quilt. Cut an 8" piece of muslin equal to that length—you may need to seam several muslin strips together to make the required length.

Fold in 1/4" on each end of the muslin strip and press. Fold again and stitch to hold. Fold the muslin strip lengthwise with right sides together. Sew along the long side to make a tube. Turn the tube right side out; press with seam at bottom or centered on the back.

Hand-stitch the tube along the top of the quilt and the bottom of the tube to the quilt back making sure the quilt lies flat (Figure 57).

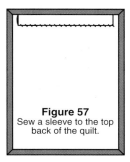

Figure 57
Sew a sleeve to the top
back of the quilt.

Stitches should not go through to the front of the quilt and don't need to be too close together.

Slip a wooden dowel or long curtain rod through the sleeve to hang.

When the quilt is finally complete, it should be signed and dated. Use a permanent pen on the back of the quilt. Other methods include

cross-stitching your name and date on the front or back or making a permanent label which may be stitched to the back.

Take a photo of your masterpiece and place with the journal you kept about the quilt. The journal should contain pieces of fabrics, dates started, the pattern used and other facts about the quilt's construction including important family and world events that influenced the hours spent working on it.

Do not tuck the quilt away in a plastic garbage bag in your cedar chest for posterity. Plastic will not let your quilt breath and it will cause damage. Store in a fabric bag in a well-ventilated area. Refold often to keep creases from forming.

The best thing to do is to use the quilt in a prominent place where everyone can see it and compliment you on a job well done.

Acknowledgments

We would like to thank the following for sharing their heirloom quilts for this book: Chris Carlson, *Patience Corner*, Page 142; Helen King, *Morning Glory*, Page 128; Helen King and Myrtle Chase, *Colonial Lady*, Page 136; Genevieve Lehman, *Dresden Plate*, Page 132; Noma Pfister, *Mother's Handkerchiefs*, Page 146; Nancy Rogerson, *T-Tulips*, Pages 90–91; Carol Scherer, *Antique Sunflower Quilt*, Page 118, *Grandmother's Choice,* Page 44, *Kaleidoscope Variation*, Page 52, *Razz-Ma-Tazz*, Page 12, *Snowball*, Page 40, *Summer Butterflies*, Page 98; Karen Schutt, *Grandmother's Square in a Square*, Page 36, *Scrappy Triangles*, Page 16; Ann Swengel, *Rose Dream Quilt,* Page 56; and Martha Wolford, *Hearts & Gizzards*, Page 114.

Special thanks to the following for photography on location: Limberlost State Historical Site, Geneva, Ind., Pages 20, 30, 62–63, 68; Roger and Naomi Muselman, Berne, Ind., Pages 84, 118, 122; Schug House Inn, Berne, Ind., Pages 6–7, 24, 90–91, 102, 108–109, 114, 128, 136; Swiss Village Retirement Community, Berne, Ind., Page 80. Dolls for photograph on Page 122 courtesy of Audrey Sullens, Fabric Creations, Crocker, Mo. Treadle sewing machine for photograph on Pages 150–151 courtesy of Robert Pyle, Bryant, Ind.